HARPETH

PRESBYTERIAN

CHURCH

1811-2011

TWO HUNDRED YEARS BESIDE THE RIVER AND THE ROAD

For Rick & Mary

Charlene Ring

Charlene Ring

2011

TABLE OF CONTENTS

INTRODUCTION

As I've often said, when I married Bob Ring, Harpeth Church came as part of the package. The home I moved into held many old Harpeth records as well as family letters and daybooks that mentioned Harpeth activities. More important, I joined a household that included Harpeth's oldest but still very active member, Bob's aunt, Emma Mai Ring. Since childhood I have been an eager listener to tales of family history, so it was natural that I continued that trait in my new home. Harpeth was an integral part of the Ring family's story.

Before my time Emma Mai Ring, Miss Genevieve Steele (mother of Lewis and Alex), Felix Treadway, Libby Friar, and Sally Lee presented historical programs or documents on our church history. Don Corlew gave Harpeth the detailed scrapbook compiled by Mary Evalyn Miller during her husband's twenty-year service to Harpeth. I have relied on all this information along with what other sources I could find at the Presbyterian Historical Foundation,, our state and county archives,, and through Google exploration. This search has been fun.

In 1976, I was asked to organize a program for our country's bicentennial in which I outlined the church's history and arranged for older members to tell of their memories. Those taped memories of Pauline Parker, Elizabeth Ring, Emma Mai Ring, Albert Merville, Bob Goodpasture and Harry Halley provide interesting insights. Others who remember attending Harpeth even occasionally

1

in the early part of the twentieth century have shared their memories with me or with Sally Lee. Sally, who attended Harpeth as young Sara Rodes in the 1950's and had some earlier memories, has shared her research with me.

And then there are~ too many to mention here~ current and recent members, some of whom "go back" before my 1963 entry. Your contributions, acknowledged along the way, give rich life to Harpeth's story.

Our pastor, David Jones, encouraged me to expand my history article, first published in Sally Lee's anthology *Beechville, Then, Now and In Between* into this book. And he took on the challenging task of preparing the manuscript for the publisher. Mary Campbell re-typed the entire text to deal with formatting issues. Carrie Jones and Kathy Simpson have been careful proof readers. Cheryl Stewart's lovely photo has been used by Mary Bowles in designing the cover.

To all of you, named and unnamed, I give thanks for helping bring this project to fulfillment. It is my hope that the recorded story of God's work in this place will not only entertain and enlighten but, more important, will challenge us to take Harpeth's mission into the future in ever more fruitful ways.

Many fine and good people have come and gone through

this old historic church on the way to heaven.

W.A. Smith

PART I

1811-1948 A COUNTRY CHURCH

Before there was a church, there was a road. And before there was a road, there was a river. The earliest travelers through the wilderness were animals and the large beasts cleared the easiest routes for all that followed – through the hills, the cane brakes, and the swamps and over the rivers. They found the best fording spot across the Little Harpeth River to be just where the Hillsboro Pike bridge is located in 2011. As time went on Native Americans of the Mississipian culture around 1200 found this a fine spot for a village. Then their culture disappeared and the natives lived here no more. They used Middle Tennessee as their "happy hunting ground". At last Europeans arrived and in their exploration and hunting they too followed these earliest paths. Samuel McCutchen and his four older brothers were among the young men who came West early to claim their rewards for having fought the British at Kings Mountain. By 1787, they were working at holding chains and guarding survey parties and learning the "lay of the land". Samuel found an ideal spot for his 640 acre grant and claimed it in September of 1784. Other than timber, much arable land, a smaller stream, and a spring, his chosen grant contained the crossing of the Little Harpeth by the rudimentary trail that led through the area. He built his home just over the hill to the south.

In 1798, the Davidson County Court ordered Samuel McCutchen and others to lay off a road from the Court House in Nashville to Ephriam Brown's on McCutchen Creek. In the 21st century this translates as " to the clubhouse at River Rest on Hillsboro Pike". Until the founding of the Nashville and Hillsborough Turnpike in 1848, maintenance of this road would have resided in the Williamson County Court which would order the landowners along its way from time to time to repair or improve it. Samuel McCutchen and his son Robert are prominent in these proceedings.

In 1809, Thomas Stockett, who had previously bought land to the east of McCutchen, bought from Samuel 2 ¼ acres of land on the river on which to build a mill. The tract was south of the river and west of the road. Because the deed refers to "the meetinghouse tract" as one of the boundaries,[i] we know that by 1809 Samuel McCutchen had set aside here at the river crossing a parcel of his land to be used for a meetinghouse. It can safely be assumed that by 1809 a small log structure stood on this spot to the northwest of the river crossing. The services of a minister would have been rare but Samuel's small building stood ready to serve when the opportunity arose. McCutchen ancestors before and sons after Samuel established Presbyterian churches wherever life took them.[ii] On a daily basis, the structure must have been a welcome shelter for travelers who stopped at this shady watering spot on the lonely road between Nashville and Hillsboro. In dry weather, it would have offered the only running water available for many miles.

One must mentally erase the modern raised roadbed and bridge in order to imagine the large shady lawn that would have extended level from the church door toward the east as far as the remnants of the old stone wall that divided McCutchen's property from Stockett's. The road would have followed that wall on the west side at this point.

Gideon Blackburn, a pioneering Presbyterian minister, moved into the Franklin area in 1810. In March of 1811 he was received into the newly created Presbytery of West Tennessee[iii] -- west then being what we now know as Middle Tennessee-- and began organizing Presbyterian churches in the area while teaching at Harpeth Academy in Franklin. Sometime in 1811 after founding First Presbyterian Church of Franklin, Gideon Blackburn established Harpeth Presbyterian Church here at the McCutchen meeting house along with four other churches in the new Presbytery. A

Gideon Blackburn, a pioneer Presbyterian minister, established Harpeth Presbyterian Church in 1811.

former student said that he preached regularly at the time for five churches within a fifty-mile radius. At Harpeth Academy, when the school bell rang on Friday he had a horse saddled and ready to start a preaching expedition.[iv] In 1814, he moved on to establish First Presbyterian Church in Nashville. We can safely assume that sometimes he preached to the little congregation at Harpeth.

Tradition says, but no deed has been found to substantiate it, that Samuel promptly deeded the land on which the church sat to the newly formed congregation. We can only guess who those founding members were. A Reverend William Hume reported that he preached both at Hermitage and at Harpeth during these early years.[v] He is said to have preached at Harpeth once a month from 1817 until the time of his death.[vi] The earliest church record we have is from 1834.[vii] It is a list of subscribers for seating and a pulpit to go in the brick sanctuary then under construction.[viii] A number of those old straight-backed pews remain in the church and in private homes. The original pulpit, though moved from the rear to the front and updated, served Harpeth continuously from the time the brick sanctuary was constructed until the flood of 2010 when it was retired to the vestibule in order to have a more spacious and versatile platform for the leading of worship. In 1835, a Rev. W.

William Hume reported that he preached at Harpeth many times during the early years.

Lapsley was paid to preach one Sunday per month for the coming year. Was the old log building still in use or was the new one already complete? We are not sure.

The new sanctuary was of bricks that had been made and fired beginning in 1830 on the farm of Samuel's eldest son, Robert McCutchen. The skilled masons created

This original pulpit and rostrum were in use continuously until 2010.

a simple but sturdy building subtly decorated with Flemish bond work under the eaves. The tall pillars that hold up the arching ceiling were set in the earth underneath the floor. Glenn Jones remembered seeing them bared at the time of the remodeling in 1949. He was not sure he remembered any stones underneath them, but he was sure that only one post showed signs of deterioration. He thought they were made from poplar heartwood. The original floor was of poplar. The pulpit originally sat between the two front doors, possibly on the same rostrum which held it until May 2010. Some of that superstructure is still below the current rostrum and its railings are in the vestibule. At the opposite end where the pulpit currently sits was a large fireplace. Windows down each side had large outdoor wooden shutters which could be closed for warmth or protection. Three of these windows were on the north side and two were on the south with a door in place of the third window facing the river, probably for bringing in wood for that large fireplace and for the entrance of slaves to the service.

The oldest session book that survives dates from March 19, 1837.[ix] The Rev. Oliver Bliss Hayes was the minister and was employed for the following year. A list of com- municants was given. Samuel McCutchen had died in 1816, but his extended

Oliver Bliss Hayes preached what we believe was the dedication service for our sanctuary in March of 1836.

family was heavily represented in the membership. Elders included David Bell, brother of Samuel's widow, as well as Samuel's sons, James and Robert. Robert lived several miles to the west on the original grant. Andrew Crockett lived in Brentwood. The church served Scots-Irish immigrants who had known one another throughout their migrations and had settled all across southern Davidson and northern Williamson Counties for miles, including children of several signers of the Cumberland Compact, namely McCutchens, Edmistons, and Crocketts.[x]

The members would have been justly pleased with this simple rectangular building with fine plastered walls and high arched ceiling – a big improvement from their former log structure. It served as the entire church for one hundred fourteen years and still serves as the sanctuary, though attached support structures have been added throughout the years. As part of those early services, communion was served from a crystal decanter and pewter cups. Robert McCutchen's wife, Martha Edmiston, would have prepared the bread and wine as she did until her death

Harpeth's original communion set consisted of this pewter cup and crystal decanter. The decanter is still in use for communion in the sanctuary.

in 1868. Responsibility for Harpeth's communion service rested with that family until the early 1900's when it passed to a cousin, Fannie Ring, and then to her daughter Emma Mai Ring, who continued to prepare the communion meal until 1974. The decanter and cups were used for many years until Harpeth was given a more "up to date" set which consisted of a silver-plated ewer with two chalices. It was given to Harpeth after Cottage Presbyterian Church of East Nashville merged with Glen Leven in 1922 and it still bears the engraving "Cottage Presbyterian Church". Sarah Parker Peay remembers taking communion at Harpeth as a teen in the early 1940's. One of the silver chalices was passed from person to person on a tray. Later at her grandmother's house, she worried about all the germs that might have been passed around on the chalice. Her mother told her that she didn't believe the Lord would let you catch something from taking Communion. From that set, the members moved to using individual cups in round wooden trays. Some of the current trays are restored from an earlier service and some are matching reproductions. In 1976 Mary Utopia Rothrock, a granddaughter of Robert and Martha Edmiston McCutchen, returned the original decanter and its pewter cups to Harpeth along with a note explaining their history. Since then the decanter has again been regularly used in Harpeth's communion service.

This communion set was "handed down" to Harpeth from Cottage Presbyterian Church in Nashville and used until individual cups came into use, probably in the 1930's.

Other than the pews and pulpit, there was one more important piece of furniture which is still at Harpeth — a tall, handsome walnut clerk's desk. It was given to Harpeth by Ellen Edmiston, wife of James McCutchen. It is made of wide walnut boards and carefully pegged together and it contains a lock. It served as the Church Office and storehouse of Sunday School material from early in the church's history until building additions were made in 1951. Those whose memories extended back into the late 1800's recalled that it sat between the two doors that led outside. (The fireplace had been closed, pot-bellied stoves installed on either side, and the pulpit moved to its current location sometime in the late 19th Century.) From 1954 until 1999 it sat in the vestibule, the first thing seen by entering worshippers. Ellen's brother, Major William Edmiston, is said to have given the first pulpit Bible.[xi] He was an interesting gentleman who had sisters and cousins who married four of Samuel McCutchen's sons. Major Edmiston doesn't seem to have ever joined the church but

This walnut clerk's desk was Harpeth's "office" for most of its history, the only repository of Sunday school materials, etc. until 1950.

he regularly supported it financially – probably at the insistence of his wife and sisters.

The Roll of 1837, transcribed here with identification,[xii] listed Elders: David Bell (half brother of Samuel's wife; married an Edmiston), Robert McCutchan, and James McCutchan, (sons of Samuel) Secretary; Members: John McCutchan (son of Samuel), Nancy McCutchan,

Elizabeth McCutchan, Mary McNeal, John F. O'Neal, Matilda O'Neal, George W. Highland, Elizabeth Wilson, Elizabeth Bell (daughter of Catherine's brother), Matilda Crockett, John Bell (son of Catherine's brother, later ran for President), Martha Bell (his sister), James Dixon (?), Catherine McCutchan (Samuel's wife), W.C. McCutchan, Martha McCutchan (son Robert's wife), Catherine McCutchan (son Robert's daughter), Mary McCutchan, Eleanor T. McCutchan, Allice Edmiston, Mary Caldwell, Robert Lazenby, Priscilla Edmiston, Jane Hey, (?) Saml. Caldwell, Cather (?) Caldwell, Mary T. Caldwell (Samuel's daughter), Wm Caldwell (Mary C.'s husband), Margaret Bell (niece of Samuel), Alpheus Bell, Andrew Crockett (husband of Samuel's niece), Cyrus G. Hulme, John Bell Sr (Catherine's half-brother)., Sarah Bell (John Sr.'s wife), Joseph Pinkerton, Elizabeth Pinkerton, Margaret Campbell, Barbara H. McCutchan (daughter of son Robert), Martha Caldwell (probably a relative of Samuel's son-in-law William Caldwell).

On September 24, 1837, Robert McCutchen was appointed to attend Synod of Tennessee at Paris, Tennessee and James McCutchan was to attend Nashville Presbytery at Franklin. These first minutes were approved at the meeting of Presbytery held in Franklin.

Ministers known from the minutes and other sources to have served in these early years were the following:

- ❖ W. Lapsley, 1835;
- ❖ O.B. Hayes, (prominent Nashville lawyer and father of Adelicia Hays Acklen) 1836 and 1837;
- ❖ William Anderson Scott (Principal of Nashville Female Academy), 1838;

- ❖ Mr. Bain and Mr. Robert Lapsley held a sacramental meeting in May of 1841. Lapsley was minister for six months of 1840.
- ❖ James H. Henderson, 1842;
- ❖ John W. Ogden, 1843-1859; There were thirty-five communicants in 1844, a low of sixteen in May of 1857.
- ❖ W.A. Harrison, assisting minister, summer 1848;
- ❖ J.W. Hoyte, 1859-1862.
- ❖ J.A. Ewing, of Pennsylvania, October 1859-February, 1860.
- ❖ W.L. Rosser, 1866.

W. L. Rosser, a Confederate soldier who stayed in the Franklin area to marry and to serve in the Presbyterian churches of the Nashville vicinity, was Harpeth's minister in 1866.

It is not likely that any of these men preached more than twice a month at Harpeth, and occasionally the service was only for each fifth Sunday! Most of them w would have been would have been serving at least one other church at the same time and possibly teaching at an area school as well. They would have traveled, at first by horseback, later by carriage, to reach the church and would have likely spent a night in the community. Services may have been in the afternoons, as we know they were later.

In the 1840's, there is first mention of contributions to the Commissioner's Fund (from Presbytery to General Assembly), Foreign and Domestic Mission Funds, the Educational Fund, and Stewart College.

During these years the number of communicants moved up and down repeatedly from the mid-thirties to the teens. Most members dismissed during this period were moving west, it seems, often to the care of The Western Presbytery. Remember that a Nashville Presbytery was formed in 1834 and Harpeth was now a part of it. The Western Presbytery now included the territory opened by the Jackson Purchase. Those early minutes record only occasional baptisms and deaths, one marriage, the appointment of ministers, and regular attendance at Presbytery. In October of 1841, Presbytery met at Harpeth. New members of note in September of 1848 were Hiram Eleazer Ring, Emma Tennessee Motheral (soon to marry H.E. Ring) and her sister America Motheral. The Motherals had been friends, neighbors, and even in-laws with the McCutchen family since before 1800. The Motheral family had earlier supported a Cumberland Presbyterian congregation nearer their home. The young Ohio school teacher, H.E.Ring..had stopped on his way home from the Mexican War to teach in the school that was then beside our church. He stole Emma Motheral's heart and, being a devout Presbyterian, must have "shown her the error of her ways".

It is assumed that slaves attended the services from the beginning. In 1848, the session minutes record receiving into membership upon examination a "collared woman Eliza belonging to Wm. Scruggs". In 1858, Rina and Peggy, servants of William Edmiston, were received on examination and baptized. In 1860, 1861, and 1865, one colored communicant is listed, no name given. There is no later reference to colored members, but black persons from the community were buried on the church property between the building and the river well into the twentieth century.[xiii]

The war years were hard on the congregation. In 1861 Elizabeth Bell died; in 1863, her husband David Bell; in 1864, James McCutchen. Both armies traveled Hillsboro Road until it was a worn mess; they sought shelter and sanctuary in our building after battles. Wounded were cared for there. It is told that America Motheral, a member of Harpeth since 1848, met her future husband, Dr. Joseph A. Bowman of Nashville, while nursing wounded there. Initials and other whittlings were left on the posts and pews by soldiers. Nearly a year after the terrible battles of Franklin and Nashville, the minutes of Harpeth report the collection of $17.65 to repair the church. Around that time, Ellen McCutchen (widow of James) wrote in a letter to a niece, "Our Church has been badly treated by the Yanks. We are having it fixed up." She described their current minister, Mr. Rosser, as "a young rebel soldier." He preached "one Sabbath in the month."[xiv]

In 1866, the Clerk of the Presbytery commented that the minutes of Harpeth were "somewhat irregular in form but they embrace in detail proceedings of the church". It is almost miraculous that the church could have continued through this period but it did. The death of James McCutchen seems to have closed an era for Harpeth Church.

James was succeeded as Clerk of the Session by his son Samuel Edmiston McCutchen. He and his mother Ellen are credited with saving papers James had carefully organized relating to the family and to Harpeth Church.[xv]

There are gaps in service records of ministers but here are most of the men who served in the pulpit of Harpeth in the period from 1866 until 1948 when it entered its modern era. Most summers protracted meetings were held and some of these ministers may have only served in that way. "Protracted meeting" was the name then used for a "revival". A visiting minister would have stayed in a member's home and preached two Sundays and the week nights between in late summer when crops were in but it was still warm and light for evening services.

- ❖ W.L. Rosser, 1866;
- ❖ N. Cunningham, 1868-1871;
- ❖ Enloe, 1873; In 1873, Ellen McCutchen died; in 1875, her son Samuel E. McCutchen died. On July 17, 1873, Elder John B. Murrey was elected to the office of Clerk of the Session, the first time this office was held by anyone other than a McCutchen.
- ❖ Rev. John Hoyte seems to have visited in September of 1873 and performed a baptism while he was there. In 1876 he appears to have been the minister
- ❖ W. Boyce Thompson served 1876-1877. In 1877, there were thirty-seven communicants. For the first time Sabbath School is mentioned with thirty children enrolled.
- ❖ R.W. Wilson served from 1878 through 1881. He was minister at Bethesda and New Hope churches south of Franklin and probably preached at Harpeth

two afternoons a month. At some point he married Nannie Byrn, a granddaughter of Robert McCutchen who had grown up in Harpeth. After her death he married Mary McClellan, sister of member Fannie McClellan Ring.[xvi] Since he was much older than she, he died only a couple of years later. Fannie Ring's husband, Henry, was elected Superintendent of the Sabbath School in 1879. In 1880, there were twenty-six commun- icants and thirty in the Sabbath School.

John B. Murrey, elected Clerk of the Session in 1873, was the first to hold this office who was not a McCutchen.

❖ Boyce Thompson preached some fifth Sundays. In 1882, he again became the regular minister but he died within the year.

❖   J.S Arbuthnot in November of 1883 began a long relationship with Harpeth until about 1900.   He is the minister remembered by Emma Mai Ring from all of her childhood. She was born in 1887 and attended Harpeth until

Memories of Harpeth: Emma Mai Ring

Now I remember. I was just a little bitty child when Dr. Arbuthnot preached but I remember him to this day for one thing. He preached in just an ordinary tone but one day got way up in a high voice, like to scared me to death; I thought the old devil was loose in the church. I looked around and then I looked up at my mother and she was perfectly calm. I got right up close to her and stayed there the rest of the day. One time my little brother (we had those wooden benches) and I don't know how in the world a little boy could turn one over, but right in the middle of the service you know he turned that bench over, and all you could see was the little feet poking up there. Now of course, my father went to his rescue immediately and put it up. The preacher stopped preaching till things settled down and we all forgot about it.   Till now I remember it. And the early preachers I think lived around Nashville, and they came out to preach to us in the afternoon. All our services in the beginning were in the afternoon and they came every other Sunday. They didn't preach every Sunday.

her death in 1986. But Dr. Arbuthnot must have been a bit lax in his organization, and the McCutchens were no longer there to keep things recorded in proper Presbyterian fashion. In 1887, it was noted by the examiner that the session had met only twice since 1881 and had not reported to the Presbytery in all those years.

We do have a few vivid recollections of the last decade of the nineteenth century. Miss Emma Mai shared her memories of Christmas at the Church. According to her, the tree at the Church was the only lighted one in the area. The entire community came to see the Children's Christmas Tree on a weeknight shortly before Christmas Day. The sanctuary would have been heated (just barely) with both large stoves and illuminated with kerosene lamps that could be lowered for lighting. I suspect this was the only night service held in the dark mid-winter. A cedar tree large enough to touch the ceiling (as least as remembered from childhood) was placed in the center front of the church and candles were carefully clamped to many of its branches and lit only for the service.

All the decorations were homemade-- garlands of colored paper, popcorn and cranberries and sometimes painted seed pods. A ladder and a large bucket of water stood nearby in case of fire. Following a simple pageant of the Christ child's birth, each child was given a gift and a fruit-filled stocking-- something only available at Christmas. Sometimes adult neighbors exchanged gifts there also. Miss Emma Mai remembered the wonder she felt at those childhood celebrations and participated in bringing that same joy to later generations of Harpeth and Beechville children. For many years her brothers took the youth out to get the tree and she supervised the youth in decorating the tree and preparing for the little children. Until she was in her eighties, she still was "honorary" director of the youth tree decoration. As long as he lived, her brother Ned Ring took pride in providing the biggest and most beautiful oranges and apples he could find.

Robert W. Wilson served Harpeth 1878 through 1881; shown here with his wife Nannie Byrn Wilson (R) and her sister Ellen Byrn Ballard (L). These women were great-granddaughters of Samuel McCutchen and had been born and reared on the McCutchen farm.

But that is getting ahead. Henry Ring's daybooks[xvii] state that they began Sunday school (after a cold winter break, it is supposed) on April 24 of 1892 and that he paid to Dr. Arbuthnot in 1892 on "Apr. 16 John Tucker 2.00 Dr. Byrn 20.00". In 1894, he mentions that Dr. Arbuthnot preached on the third Sunday of each month. In 1895 and again in 1897, the Session appointed committees to inquire into the whereabouts of five hundred dollars left to the church by

James McCutchen in his will,[xviii] the interest therefrom to help pay the cost of ministers. An existing receipt shows that John Murrey had paid one hundred dollars of it to R.W. Wilson in 1882. In 1887, Henry Ring, Emma Mai's father, became an

Memories of Harpeth: Emma Mai Ring

But we had Sunday School every Sunday. And we had our Sunday School right in this room. And so far as I remember we had three classes. And the older folks up here and then the younger people on that side and the children way back there in the back. And as far as I know all of us here in one room, so far as I know, there never was any disturbance from the little children. They were as quiet as they could be, and they had their lesson, and they had their catechism and we all, we older folks, we had gone through the catechism and we had learned it. That was a thing we had every Sunday, the catechism. And the little children had the Child's Catechism and we had the Shorter Catechism.

Elder. Rev. Angus McDonald and Rev. R.W.Wilson served in addition to Dr. Arbuthnot in 1899. In that year, trustees were elected for the first time. Joseph Bowman, son of America Motheral Bowman and ward of the Rings, John Tucker and George Kinnie were elected and instructed to meet with John Murrey about the funds that had been bequeathed to Harpeth by James McCutchen at his death in 1864. Henry Ring was now Clerk of the Session. No result of the investigations was ever reported in any session minutes.

In fact records are missing from 1899 until 1914! Nashville Presbytery history fills in some of this period. Harpeth's minute book exists but there are many blank pages, indicating that the minutes were not misplaced but never recorded.here. In 1900, R.W. Wilson was at Harpeth as Supply while serving as Superintendent of Monroe Harding Children's Home.[xix] There is also reference to a Mr. Ham as interim.

Memoirs of members such as Emma Mai Ring and Pauline Parker make clear that members met at the church on Sunday afternoon whether or not there was a minister and had a lesson and singing.

The Rev. G. B. Harris, Jr. wrote a record of his ministry at Harpeth which extended from 1906 until 1921.[xx] Lewis Collins' letters and comments from church members indicate his interest in youth – a quality not always evident in some of these earlier ministers. But if they only appeared for part of a day once or twice a month, what could they have been expected to provide for youth, other than to make their sermons interesting for them? In early 1907, Harris was again asked and did preach at Harpeth from April of 1907 with some regularity. He tells that they usually "began services in the Spring and held regularly until Winter, when no more services were held until the following spring." When he was not the Stated Supply he would hold the "protracted meeting" in the summer. "I was met at the end of the (then new) Bellemeade car-line, by old 'Uncle Chester', - an old darkey who used to drive me back to Nashville, in the West

Side days. I would take dinner… at Capt. Harrison's and then drive on to Harpeth, and after service, the old darkey would drive back to the car-line." Harris served as a Chaplain in WWI during which time he visited and preached at

Memories of Harpeth: Pauline Parker

Now this church building was located on this spot which was level with the road outside. Big locust trees stood in the churchyard and stones marked the graves of slaves outside the church here. I so well remember the two wood burning stoves placed on each side of the room – they were the fat rectangular type with a little platform in front and a door in which you pushed the wood that was used for refueling. These stoves were later replaced with one big coal burning stove which was placed over there on the south side. And in the winter we all gathered round close to that old stove. Miss Ellen Byrn was my first Sunday school teacher- that I remember. We had the little picture cards with the title and the golden text and story printed on the back. We loved those little cards.

Harpeth three times. Next he served at Wartrace, much farther away, but he still managed to preach at Harpeth every fifth Sunday. He concluded, "I have been connected with Harpeth Church, now, at various times, since April 1906- more than 15 years. I was the regular Stated Supply, or acting

Pastor from April 1907-1909, and from July 1913 – September of 1917, - in all a period of 6 years. In the 10 years from 1907 to 1917, I did practically all the preaching that was done in the church". His service included 143 sermons, 4 Communions, 3 baptisms, 3 funerals, 2 marriages, 1 ordination, 4 members received, and 162 visits."[xxi]

Mr. Millard, who was minister at New Hope and Bethesda, is mentioned as preaching in 1912. In 1913, J.T. Rothrock, then living in Memphis, wrote to thank Fannie Ring for her hospitality during his recent visit to "Beachville" where the letter indicates he had held a "protracted meeting". Rothrock first married Utopia Ada Herron, and after her

W.C. Alexander, full time pastor of Glen Leven Presbyterian Church, offered his services to Harpeth for occasional afternoon services and for sacramental needs during these hard years.

death married her cousin Tennessee Byrn. Both women were grandchildren of Robert McCutchen. As rural population continued to shrink during these years, Harpeth was affected. At least one member, Frank Ring, now slept in a cemetery in France.

W.C. Alexander, pastor of Glen Leven Church in Nashville and possibly a relative of some Harpeth members, helped out at a time when

The church building here reflects these lean and hard years.

the church almost closed by preaching there on Sunday afternoons after his Glen Leven services. In 1925, he officiated at the marriage of Suzanne Elizabeth Ring to Edward Uehling in the Ring home, and, in 1929, he baptized their son Edward at Harpeth.[xxii] This may have been a favor to relations as well as ministry to the congregation. In 1930, Henry Ring died, leaving J. H. Allen as the sole elder.

The Rev. W.L. Smith was called as pastor for a salary of $250 per year in September of 1931. Dr. Alexander moderated Harpeth's meeting. Mr. Smith noted six years later when he was still receiving the same salary, "This is $15 per member which is very good, considering the few who can give. Our spiritual birth rate is low tho, only 3%."[xxiii] In another report he stated, " Many fine and good people have come and gone through this old historic church on the way to heaven." Mr. Smith also served Bethesda and New Hope churches in Williamson County. He preached every other Sunday afternoon at Harpeth having supper in one of the homes from 1931 through 1946. The membership during his tenure grew from 20 to a high of 31, usually staying around 25. Session minutes were regularly kept. Sunday school, Bible school, and women's Bible study classes were held regularly. This small congregation

W. L. Smith, Harpeth's beloved pastor from 1931 through 1946.

managed to bring in almost 40 children to Bible school every summer during these years. Emma Mai Ring had by now been teaching at nearby Grassland School for many years and she no doubt had a hand in finding and bringing those children.

Mr. Smith was a humble man, by his own admission not a strong speaker. Members recalled that he spoke not from the pulpit but down front, on the level of his small congregation. Ned Uehling, who often attended during his years as a Vanderbilt student, recalled that Mr. Smith was "a tall, thin, soft spoken gentleman...an intelligent man and his wife was a graduate of Columbia University, a fact occasionally mentioned by [my] grandmother or [aunt] with perhaps a twinge of envy." The '30's were marked by the building of the new U.S. highway across the church's front lawn. At first there had been no bridge, only a ford, which had been the reason for the locating of the church on this site in the first place. In addition to the coming of the road, there was a problem with a neighbor who was 'camping out' on the church grounds trying to establish his right to the property. Mr. Smith's correspondence shows that considerable effort was expended in 1933 defending against this threat.[xxiv] G. B. Harris' accounting of his service was compiled to show that the church had indeed continued to meet actively during those years. The original 'deed' from Samuel McCutchen to the church had never been recorded and was never found. Much work had to be done to establish the lines legally.[xxv] In 1937, Ned Ring

A Smith era Vacation Bible School, probably around 1943. Teachers are Blanche Parker (L) and Emma Mai Ring ®. Among the pupils are Jackie Holt (Orand) and Ned Vehling.

and Earl Carter became Elders. In 1938, the leaders were discussing the necessity of building up the driveway to meet the new higher road and they met on a Saturday in January to do the work. In 1939, the trustees were instructed to represent the church in settling its land boundaries and its damages incident to the new bridge and highway construction. In 1946, Rev. Smith left Harpeth, Bethesda, and New Hope to accept a call in Kentucky.

Memories of Harpeth: Elizabeth Moran Ring and Sam Moran

Elizabeth Moran Ring: And this church was clean for the services. I'm not gonna call names but I'm sure a lot of you knew --. Well, he claimed this property and he resented us being here and resented us having services. So one night I was sittin' right over there by that window for the night services and he got up right outside that window and he was kinda drunk and he mumbled and fussed and mumbled and fussed and I want you to know that I did not hear another word of that sermon. I expected a bullet to come right through that window just any minute. I never was so scared. I never will forget that as long as I live.

Sam Moran: I remember the congregation being Parkers, Rings, Kinnies and the Allens and that Mr. Smith was minister. Mr. Smith ate lunch with the Parkers and supper with the Rings or vice-versa. Cousin Sallie Byrn Kinnie played the little pump organ and Mr. Allen led the singing. When I listen to those songs so slow now, I remember Mr. Allen going so fast that Miss Sallie had to 'pump like hell' to keep up with him. Mr. Allen was superintendent of the grounds at Percy Warner Park. He brought all the workers with him. I suppose maybe Mr. Allen made them come.

C.N. Ralston next filled this Sunday afternoon position at Harpeth while dividing his Sunday mornings between Bethesda and New Hope. Harpeth's membership was dwindling but Ralston is credited with having the vision that Harpeth should be prepared for a new role as a suburban church. He recognized that the area around it was already beginning to change as Nashville grew southward. And he carried that vision to the Presbytery. Ralston himself was in poor health but he managed to inspire

Probably early 1940's. Electric service had come. The sign and the light above it must have been attempts to counteract the feeling that the world was swiftly passing them by on the new raised roadway and bridge.

action. Lewis Steele had grown up at Bethesda and still had ties in that church and community. He was now a successful businessman and an Elder at Westminster Presbyterian Church in Nashville. He and his wife Annie began spending their Sunday afternoons teaching Sunday School at Harpeth and doing a bit of 'moving and shaking' in the background.

PART II

NEW MISSION FOR AN OLD CHURCH

1948-1969

In the fall of 1948 C.N. Ralston, assisted by Lewis Steele, presented to the Session and members of Harpeth a plan: Ralston resigned and the Rev. Priestley Miller, formerly a Methodist minister, was called to be Harpeth's first full time pastor. He accepted the call and his service began October 3, 1948. Behind the scenes, it had been arranged that a group of laymen in Nashville would supplement his salary. The Presbytery and Harpeth agreed for a six-month 'trial'.[xxvi] That was the beginning of a twenty-year marvel. The Presbytery met at

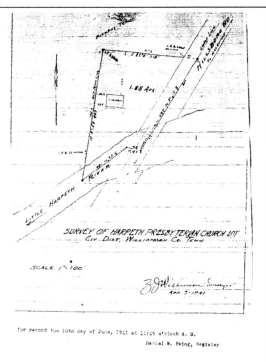

1941 Plat showing the land remaining after the State road and bridge were built in the 1930's.

Harpeth for Miller's installation on November 11, 1948. The bulletin provided by Presbytery, no doubt the first at Harpeth, stated that WOC (Women of the Church) would soon be organizing and that Young People and Young Adults of the community would meet at the home of Battle and Sara Rodes on Saturday evening, December, 4, for fun and

Priestley Miller, God's instrument for leading the transformation of Harpeth from a small struggling country congregation into a vibrant suburban one.

recreation. Madison P. Jones with his wife Mary and their sons,[xxvii] Glenn and Madison, were the first new members after Miller came. Madison, known usually as Percy, had been among the businessmen agreeing to support Harpeth. Jones had helped found McCarthy Jones and Woodard Steel Fabrication in Nashville and was at that time its president. Interestingly, he now owned the former McCutchen farm and occupied that home which had sheltered so many of Harpeth's stauncher members. Mary Jones invited a group of about thirty community women to lunch in her home and had a lady from Glen Leven Church explain the work of the Presbyterian WOC. She accepted the presidency of the group and they got busy! The church had only a very dirty and worn sanctuary – no Sunday school rooms, no kitchen, no restroom! This group held bake sales, ice cream suppers, box suppers, and rummage sales to make money. They donned work clothes to scrub and paint the old original gray pews gleaming white. It was a time of close Christian working fellowship for a loyal few.

Mary Temple Jones

Through the years Mary Temple Jones served in all offices of the WOC and ably recorded the church's annual history. She was a great visitor for the church bringing in many new members.

Earlier in 1948, Harpeth reported a membership of twenty-two with four elders. As Miller began his work there were eighteen attendees in three Sunday School classes, children taught by Earl Carter, youth taught by Emma Mai Ring, and adults taught by Pauline Parker. Madison Jones started a second adult class which met in his home. Other members who came in early were the Lewis Steele family, who had been attending for several years, Bob and Helen Goodpasture, Bob and Roberta Alexander, and the Keenan Foster, B.K. Hibbett, and John Jeffords families.

Though the Battle Rodes family never formally moved their membership from West End Methodist, they were deeply involved and supportive. They had a large room in their home, across Hillsboro Road from the Jones' home. The called it "The Great Hall" and in addition to entertaining their friends, they offered it to many organizations. The Harpeth women took their sewing machines there and sewed massive drapes for its openings, earning money for renovations and making the hall a more comfortable place for the many church functions, including Easter sunrise services, that would be held there while the little building was being renovated--and later.

The men organized

Harpeth Presbyterian Church
ORGANIZED 1811

SERVICES EACH SUNDAY MORNING AT 11:00 A.M.
SUNDAY SCHOOL AT 10:00 A.M.
REVEREND PRIESTLEY MILLER, Pastor

LOCATED ON HILLSBORO ROAD JUST SOUTH OF OLD HICKORY BLVD.   NASHVILLE, TENNESSEE

This bulletin of August 17, 1949, was the first for regular use. Designed and donated by Keenan Foster, it featured a photo of the cleaned up but so far basically unchanged building.

the cleanup, tearing out the old poplar floors which had holes large enough to catch a woman's shoe heel. They cleaned, re-paired, and painted the walls that had the residue of many floods that had risen to pew level. They cleaned out the coal bin that had been kept in one corner for the pot-bellied

Memories of Harpeth: Bob Goodpasture and Albert Merville

Bob Goodpasture: I remember we had a service down there one Sunday, and Mr. Ned [Ring] brought a great big ham. I guess it weighed 50 pounds. We had a picnic in that old building. That was when I first came down and some woman got her heel hung in the floor. Well, it was old boards; they had to pull the plank up and take her shoe off to get it loose

Albert Merville: …if you had any religion when you came in here at 11 then you'd lost it when you left. (speaking about the old benches)

stoves, the heat source that had replaced that original fireplace. They paid to have modern heating installed and a new floor put in professionally, and, like the women, they bonded as a Christian fellowship as they rolled up their sleeves and worked together. Outside, they removed the bedraggled wooden shutters from the windows and the large sign from above the front door and they groomed the churchyard.

For the Easter service April 17, Keenan Foster donated Harpeth's first bulletin. He and his family lived around the corner on Old Hickory Boulevard and he worked for Clement Paper Company. On August 17, regular use of

Memories of Harpeth: Buck (Glenn) Jones

Buck(Glenn) Jones is the grandson of Madison and Mary Temple Jones, the son of Glenn and Mary Jones. Born in 1948, he grew up in Harpeth and as an adult was a session member and an active leader until he moved to Tampa, Florida, with his wife Mary Jane and sons Madison and Logan. He recalls that his grandparents never went out on Saturday night because that was when Mr. Jones prepared his Sunday School lesson. He would light a cigarette and set it on the edge of the table. When one side of the table got too many burns on it, he would give the table a quarter turn until it was burned all around at which time he'd get a new card table.

bulletins began. They featured a photo of the cleaned up but as yet basically unchanged building. Until his death Foster produced Harpeth's bulletins.

In October, 1949, a Hammond organ arrived for Mary Evalyn Miller, our minister's wife, to play. Helen Goodpasture and the Alexanders had led in the fund-raising for it. Harpeth's ladies made and donated items that were sold in a Fall Market at Roberta Alexander's Hillsboro Knit Shop in Nashville. This organ replaced an old reed organ that had been in use since the late 1800's. Miss Pauline

Parker remembered Sallie Byrn Kinnie playing that organ while Pauline stood beside it singing with an afternoon Sunday School class that sometimes included only Mr. Ring, his son Andrew, and Mr. James. Allen. Miss Parker took the old organ to her school and had it refurbished. Her niece now owns it.

By the fall of 1949, Bob Goodpasture had completed a brick terrace and walk in front of the church. Glenn Jones remembered the men sitting on the patio (probably smoking) and brainstorming about what the church needed.

This small reed organ served Harpeth from the late 1800's until 1949. Miss Pauline Parker, who offered her rich contralto voice to Harpeth's service throughout her life, asked to have it when it was replaced. She restored it as shown here.

Memories of Harpeth: Sara Rodes and Ruth Steele

Sara Rodes: When Priestley came and welded together the members, old and new and the neighbors as friends of Harpeth, it was a great step forward and achievement. And then Mary Evalyn came and brought a program of lovely music, which was unequaled anywhere and she contributed to the Church the finest music program ever - and for a small church. When remodeling came on, they met at our house, and it did something for us and for our house to have them – Easter, Christmas, Easter Breakfast after the Easter service at the church. We felt it a great honor to have Harpeth meet at our home. We felt that our house had been blessed and it was a better place to live in. The suppers and lunches we have had with you are a part of our religious and neighborhood life. And now Sally and John are here and our grandchildren are growing up in your church – Our church.

Ruth Steele: One Sunday afternoon, Alex and I were invited to come to a Sunday School class which met in the Sanctuary at 2:00. Miss Emma Mai was the teacher and led the discussion. There were eight to ten in the class. We enjoyed it very much. After Alex and I left, I said, "Well, Alex, with that eager bunch, and as energetic as they are, and as determined as they are to have a church, we can at least go and warm 18-20 inches of bench every Sunday. That was 1947.

Memories of Harpeth: Sally Lee

I can remember we gathered at the house- you know it's often cold- but we were gonna have the service outside on the brow of the hill so you could look out over the valley; they were going to sort of walk out to the middle of that and sit on some benches and you don't quite see Harpeth Church from there but almost. And one time we were going to dress the girls as Easter angels and we had white robes. We used to go and buy great bolts of cloth. They were very simple robes. And we got down there that morning and dressed them for the first time. They had practiced – and every girl had on a pink dress and the pink glowed through the white and it was just great. We didn't plan it that way; it just happened and so it glowed in the sunrise; it was really nice. And see, when they had the sunrise service. We'd have breakfast in the Great Hall after the sunrise service, we'd have, I don't know what you call it but it is hard boiled eggs in cream sauce. So you could do the hard boiled eggs the day before or sometimes you'd just have hard boiled eggs dyed but sometimes you have them shredded in cream sauce and pour it over biscuits…And so Mrs. Provine came out with a huge thing of eggs. They were too small to sell and she brought them all over for us to use for the sunrise service…..

By now the Bill Halley family was attending and the first Rally Day had been held. Prayer meeting was on Wednesday nights, and fellowship suppers were held on the first Thursday of each month. Men of the Church and other groups met on other Thursday

The interior front during the marriage of Linda Jean Irwin (Linda Woodside) and David C. Crockett, October 2, 1950. Notice the old original pews.

nights. On November 20, 1949, just a year after Priestley Miller's installation, a Building Fund was begun, the first gift coming from the children and youth. There were now 16 attending Youth Fellowship. In the winter they had a box supper to make money for the Building Fund. Every first Sunday offering would go to the Building Fund. The ladies had an Easter Food Market at Roberta Alexander's knit shop. A well was dug on the property before the building construction began. Dr. McNeil of Scotland led a revival in the summer. Due to crowding, the adult Sunday School classes took turns meeting in homes – Jones or Rodes. In November, Emma Mai Ring, Mrs. R.W. Ratliff and Lewis Steele were securing furnishings for the new rooms. Bessie and Margaret Sawyer joined Harpeth that fall, as did the Hydes. The youth put on a Christmas pageant led by their president, Sally Rodes. It was the first of many original pageants Sally would provide for Harpeth holidays, in her youth and later when her own children were there as participants.

Work on the wrap-around addition was ongoing throughout 1950. On September 29, 1950, Harpeth hosted the wedding of Jean Irwin and David C. Crockett.

Annie Steele soloist and Mary Evalyn Miller organist on Harpeth's new Hammond organ.

Though there are records of marriages being performed by past ministers, there is no clear evidence that a 'formal' wedding had ever before been performed in the church building. Most would have been held in homes or perhaps in conjunction with "sacramental meetings".

Jean Irwin grew up on the John Sugg farm where her father managed the dairy. She had been brought throughout her youth to Sunday school and Bible school by her teacher at Grassland School, Emma Mai Ring, and she was a girl the women of Harpeth came to love and respect. They gave her this wedding-- and I am sure they found joy not only in giving to her but also in dressing up their newly cleaned and decorated sanctuary for the first time.

Prior to the wedding, bridesmaids gathered at the John Sugg home (where Murray Lane meets

Bride and groom stand before the rostrum and pulpit.

Hillsboro Road) to get dressed. Mr. and Mrs. Lewis Steele saw that the church was decorated with ferns, mums, and candles by Truett Floral in Franklin. In the rear of the church there was a food table on the left and a table for gifts on the right.

Mary Evalyn Miller played the organ, Annie Steele sang and Priestley Miller officiated. Following the ceremony guests were served cake and punch that had been prepared by the women of the church.

Since then, Harpeth has seen many, many weddings.[xxviii] Guidelines for weddings at Harpeth have had to be revised many times in order to avoid Harpeth being used as just a pretty little wedding chapel. Our guidelines requiring membership and counseling have often led young couples to stay and start their families here.

Reception in rear of sanctuary: Nell Ring right foreground, groom's twin brother, Madison Jones, Mary Evalyn Miller, Winifred Halley, Annie Steel, server unidentified.

The wrap around wing was completed in February of 1951. An open house in March included the setting of a cornerstone. Membership was now fifty-eight. This new addition provided a fellowship hall to the south of the sanctuary, bathrooms, a kitchen, a nursery, and a connecting hall behind the sanctuary, and an office and Pastor's study to the north of the sanctuary. There was plumbing and a real heating plant. Keenan Foster gave an air conditioner for the pastor's study. Upstairs there were several Sunday school rooms. The men involved remembered until the day they died moving the upright piano up those steep narrow steps. All this space called for an expanded Church School staff. While they were doing all this, the congregation was recognized for leading the Presbytery and perhaps the General Assembly in per capita giving![xxix]

Memories of Harpeth: Elizabeth Ring

(Speaking on New Benches) You couldn't mess around with Mr. Miller. If you mentioned anything and made a suggestion to Mr. Miller, well then, you got appointed chairman and told to go ahead and do it. So they were with us at Mrs. Ring's one night and Emma Mai and Nell [Mrs. James E. Ring] were talking and said something about we needed some new benches. We, he said "All right, I appoint you a committee and you can go ahead and work them up." And they did; they got some more people on it. And each family in the church gave a seat. And we have a lot of good neighbors, like Mr....over here and he gave us one. And one of the members of our church at that time had given a good deal of money for another purpose and he could not buy a seat but he said "Well, that's all right. For me and my house, we'll sit on Mr....."s seat for I know he'll never come and use it."

There was summer fellowship on the lawn followed by singing inside afterward. A committee to raise money for new pews was formed. Most church families bought one new pew and in return took an old one home. B. K Hibbett, chairman of the committee, bought four and succeeded in getting several businesses to pay for one. In August our sign, the one that stands beside the office entrance now, was erected at our highway entrance – a gift of the Nashville Ornamental Iron Works, arranged by Bob Goodpasture. On

December 30, 1951, the bulletin had a new cover showing the wrap-around addition, the front terrace and brick walk.

Building Committee for wrap-around addition: Bob Alexander, Bob Goodpasture, Lewis Steele, Pastor Priestley Miller, Madison Jones, Ned Ring.

In 1952, the March membership count was up to sixty-eight. Fellowship suppers were moved to Wednesday evenings before prayer meeting and singing. The WOC met at the church twice a month. Bob Goodpasture was working on landscaping. On April 13, the new pews were used for the first time. On April 27, the choir sang for the first time at Harpeth. You see, a bonus that came with Priestley Miller was his ability as a tenor and choir director and his wife Mary Evalyn's talent as accompanist. He directed the choir and occasionally sang tenor solos until his death. Mary Evalyn continued as organist for some years after.

Seven of our youth went to NaCoMe – our church's Tennessee retreat ground named for the three Presbyteries it served – <u>Na</u>shville, <u>Co</u>lumbia, and <u>Me</u>mphis. The WOC began its ongoing practice of providing some scholarships to NaCoMe. They raised money by serving lunches at the nationally known purebred cattle sales held every year at the Jones' Harpeth Valley Farm. They also began a White Cross group that met at the church to roll bandages and make clothes for the Korean mission field or for the Martha O'Bryan Settlement House. They provided suppers for the youth group. Sally Rodes wrote and directed her third

Memories of Harpeth: Pauline Parker

One day I needed to go to the church around noon for something and since there was a highway worker parked there for his lunch break, I tried to look like I was just going around so he wouldn't suspect I was getting the key. After a bit, the man called out, "Ma'am, if you're looking for the key, they keep it under that rock on the step".

Memories of Harpeth: Laura Dreher

[On Mr. Alex Bright] I have very distinct memories of people who made Harpeth our home. First was Mr. Alex. He was the custodian and was a friend to everyone. When I was little, adults were big and a little intimidating to talk to, but Mr. Alex was always so kind and easy to talk to. He always seemed to care and be interested in what I was saying. He really taught me through his actions.

Christmas pageant. At year's end the membership had grown to 80 and the indebtedness had been reduced by $7000.

In 1953, they began having flowers in the sanctuary every Sunday. Membership grew to 100. A night circle of young women was organized. The debt for the first addition was paid off and plans were being made for a vestibule and bell tower.

By 1954 the membership 125. The Joe Dickinson family, the Moores, Burroughs, Everharts and many others joined. A second sewing machine had been bought for the church and White Cross produced fifty-two garments and one hundred seventy compresses. The first of many Gay Nineties events was a picnic supper on the church lawn. For this event senior citizens from Martha O'Bryan Center in Nashville were transported to Harpeth for an evening of entertainment and very good eating.

Winter, about 1952. Notice the chimney and the fence and trees that defined our property line just behind the addition.

The tradition continued until the early Nineties with a large bus eventually being required to bring the expanding group. The bell tower was completed. The bell was donated by Battle and Sara Rodes in honor of their daughter Sally's graduation from college. Sally once again directed the Christmas pageant. Screens were placed on each side of the pulpit in front of the choir for a neater appearance. Coat racks were installed in the new vestibule. The ladies asked permission to put a 50 x 50 fenced playground southwest of the building so that children could play in a protected area during the service. Amazingly there was opposition by one of the prominent grandfathers, but the women finally prevailed. There was frequent mention of the noise coming from the nursery located immediately behind the sanctuary or

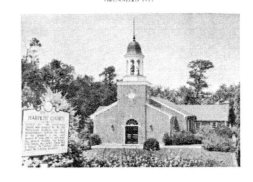

Harpeth

Presbyterian Church

ORGANIZED 1941

HILLSBORO ROAD
South of Old Hickory Blvd.
NASHVILLE, TENNESSEE
PRESBYTER MILLER, Pastor

Addition of the vestibule and bell tower altered the church's appearance dramatically. The architects reputedly chose a look borrowed from Presbyterian churches on the campus of Princeton University and in Scotland.

through open windows from the playground in summer. Women who took their turns keeping the nursery have some lively stories to tell of trying to keep the noise in check. New homes were being built in the neighborhood and the session was talking of bringing in these families and of needing once again to expand the facilities. A supper on the grounds raised money for our first choir robes, black with white collars. Another supper on the grounds and lunch at a Jones' cattle sale funded playground equipment. The WOC donated toward improving the landscaping. Bob Goodpasture was busy building the low brick wall that still defines the borders of our drive. TVA was acquiring its easement along our river bank.

A late afternoon dinner on the grounds , about 1954

*Side of the educational building showing a brick walk from the drive
and across to the main building. Playground and river are in the
distance.*

By 1955, membership had grown to 155. Our youth
entertained all the youth of our Presbytery. VBS had 29
attendees. Sadly one of several floods got up to the pew
racks inside the sanctuary. Bob Goodpasture, who was a
landscape architect for the state, was instrumental in getting
the state to build the first levee, which protected us from
flooding until the mid 1970's. We had extended west to our
property line and could not expand until we acquired more
property. Lewis Steele was able to get an additional 1.61
acres paralleling our property at an actual cost of $5000. Ned
Ring resigned as Clerk of the Session, having held that office
for more than fifteen years. Alex Steele was chosen to
succeed him. Keenan Foster died and the adult Sunday
School class that met in the parlor was named for him; his
picture hung in the parlor for a long time. His death brought

to an end his production of the bulletins; Harpeth finally had to buy its own mimeograph machine!

In 1956, James Carter, who had grown up at Harpeth during its smaller days, entered the ministry and was studying at Austin Seminary in Texas[xxx]. In the following years several young men considered going into the ministry. Mr. Miller was out of service for several months following the first of several heart attacks.

By 1957, the membership had reached 164. McKays and Hicks were among the new families. We had outgrown our first addition of educational and recreational facilities and a new building program was under way. We were desperate for air conditioning but could not get a permit. WOC had two day circles and were planning to re-start a night circle. In 1958, they provided a nursery for the day circles and bought items for the new church kitchen and antique brass vases for the sanctuary. Some of the women were still involved in Auxiliary White Cross sewing. They worked joyfully to provide whatever was asked for the mission field – from hospital gowns and clothing to bandages. And they poured their hearts into dressing Christmas dolls for little girls at Martha O'Bryan.[xxxi]

Memories of Harpeth: Beth McKay

When my family and I came to Harpeth in the late 1950's there was a very active youth group. I was in the "Pioneers", a group for seventh and eighth graders. My sister, Bonnie, was in the "Seniors", the group for ninth through twelfth graders. Fifth and sixth graders were in the "juniors". All three groups met together each Sunday evening for a light supper (provided by different members of the congregation) an opening activity with hymns accompanied by the Reverend Mr. Priestley Miller, and study sessions in individual groups led by the adult sponsors. Mr. Steele was the Pioneer's leader. We would always sing at least one hymn sometimes accompanied by Donald or Lewis Steele, Jr. or Mr. Miller. Mr. Steele sang with gusto even though he knew he was a monotone. His theory was that he was singing God's praises so the tune mattered not. We were also expected to recite a Bible verse. When I became a "Senior" I can remember several couples who helped - Martha and George Gaines, Bess and Bill Hicks, Elizabeth and Steve Blackburn, Sr.

Memories of Harpeth: Beth McKay (cont'd)

My parents, Gibson and Porter McKay, worked with the "Juniors", and June and Leonard Mika were also active during that time.

There were between 40 and 50 youth who regularly attended the Youth fellowship. Many were not associated with Harpeth except through the Youth Group. Each Sunday afternoon, Mr. Lewis Steele would make two or three trips picking up anyone interested in participating. It was the "in" thing to do!

One of our favorite activities was the annual "Possum Hunt". We would meet late in the afternoon at the Dickinson's farm to hunt 'possum. Of course, Mr. Steele always made sure we had some hot dogs just in case we were unsuccessful in our quest! The hunt ended with a big bonfire and wiener roast. The scariest hunt was the year Alex Bright, the sexton, and his friends brought along their dogs and actually caught a 'possum! Hot dogs never looked so good!!!

The theft of the church's typewriter in 1956 brought home the fact that our building was very vulnerable. A lock box was rented for papers. Through the years there have been sporadic break-ins, usually for office or electronic machines and to search for the cash that has never been kept there. One thief took the antique pulpit chairs, however. In spite of these break-ins a key was kept under a stone by the office door for many years – and this system proved our neighborhood trustworthy. None of the thieves used the key.

In October of 1958, the first part of the separate educational building was completed. It included a kitchen and fellowship hall, men's and women's restrooms, and classrooms upstairs.[xxxii] Bids were opened on the second part. The existing building was repainted inside and out. A brick walk was laid between the old and new buildings and the driveway and expanded parking lot were oiled, thanks to Bob Goodpasture. This marked exactly ten years under the leadership of Priestley Miller and dramatically demonstrated the growth of Harpeth's ministry in this period. By 1959, the membership had reached 200. Alex Steele Jr. was a

Exit from the 1951 kitchen leading across to the new educational building.

Alex Bright had lived in the Beechville community all his life. In 1959, he became sexton of Harpeth and served in that position until his retirement shortly before his death in 1978.

communicant; Bob Ring finished college and moved his membership here. Alex Bright was hired as sexton. He had lived in the neighborhood all his life and told of caring for the horses of attendees at Harpeth's services when he was young. Alex served Harpeth with loyalty and dignity for many years. As long as he was able he was groundskeeper, janitor, brass polisher – and on Sunday and other special occasions he was truly Sexton in his neat white coat. Further, he helped to forge a tie of fellowship between his congregation, Greater Pleasant View Baptist Church, and Harpeth. In 1959, the WOC presented the church with the brass tips for the candelabra and white paraments for the communion table, pulpit, and Bible. The Young Adult class gave books.

Memories of Harpeth: Beth McKay

I began singing in the choir when I was 15 years old. For a while Mr. Miller had me sing with the junior choir even though I was a little too old because they needed more voices. At one point I was asked to lead the junior choir, which I did for several years with the help of Mabeth Blackburn who played the piano for us. Mr. Miller was the choir director until his death in January of 1969. He would lead the worship service, sing with the choir and often sang a solo as well! Bob Ragan was a bass in the choir who had a very deep voice. Mr. Miller would rewrite the music an octave lower for Bob. Many years later, we had another bass with a very low voice-Don Gorman. He could use the music written for Bob Ragan. Don usually sang the bass part an octave lower anyway.

My parents, Gibson and Porter McKay, were youth advisors for the fifth and sixth graders. Mother taught and Daddy kept his thumb on the active boys who always wanted to play poker with him. Daddy was active in the Men's Club and cooked many of the monthly dinners for them. Mother started a young adult Sunday School class which she taught for several years. Annie Steele and Mother were the first women deacons at Harpeth.

1963 CHOIR: Front: Pauline Parker, Annie Steele, Leigh Anne Burrough,, Shirley Tomlin, Marie Burrough, Middle Row: Bonnie McKay, Beth McKay, Annie Carter, Back: Bob Ragan, Donald Steele, Bill Halley

1964:CHOIR: Front: ?, Bill Halley, Annie Steele, Beth McKay, Elizabeth Gaines, Marie Burrough, Back: Richard Halley, ?, Bob Ragan, George Gaines, Honey Kennedy, Harry Halley, Mary Evalyn Miller at Organ

*1962 Children's Choir: Richard Halley,
Donald Steele, Alex Steele, Sally Temple
Jones, et. Al.*

In 1960, ,work moved forward with completing theEducational Building. Membership rose to 248. The Sugg Hicks, Bradley, Williamson and Williams families joined. The Senior Highs furnished the worship center for the Educational Building with a wooden cross,[xxxiii] runners, and bookshelves. Albert Merville donated the beautiful Reredos . That is the wooden paneling and lighted cross behind the pulpit. Other denominations were buying land in the neighborhood and we were moving ahead with our expansion.

In response to the possibility of civil rights activity coming to our door, the Session voted that "should we have Colored visitors for Church Services that the Ushers be requested to seat them at the front of the church." They also voted that only literature approved by the Session be distributed on the church premises. We did have such visitors several times without incident except that we lost a small number of our members who did not wish to accept them.

On October 15, 1961, Harpeth celebrated the 150th anniversary of our founding, the 125th year in our sanctuary, the thirteenth anniversary of our reorganization under Priestley Miller, and the Centennial of the Presbyterian Church in the United States.[xxxiv] We were one of the one hundred churches over one hundred years old featured in the book, *Look to the Rock,* commemorating the PCUS Centennial. Harpeth marked the occasion with a special afternoon service followed by an Open House. Phase II of the Educational Building had been completed adding five classrooms as well as space for other purposes.

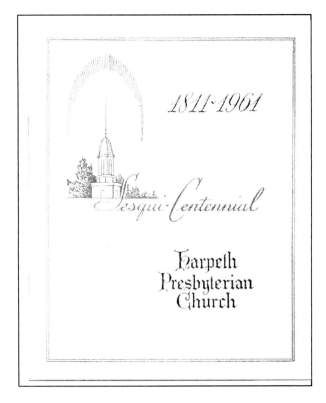

This freed space in the first addition for a secretary's office and a library. Libby Fryer organized the library largely funded then and later by the WOC. She also researched and presented a history of Harpeth to the WOC. Communicants included Harry and Richard Hally and Sally Temple Jones, children of families who had helped with the revitalization of Harpeth. The passing that year on June 24 of Ned Ring was noted; he had been a ruling elder since 1937 and was Clerk of the Session from 1938 until 1955.

As 1962 began, a slight drop in membership and attendance was noted and the session was canvassing Williamson County's first subdivision, Meadowgreen Acres, as it had already been doing in southern Davidson County. March 7, 1962 saw the publication of the first edition of *The Harpeth Newsletter*. In 1965 it became *Harpeth News Bulletin*; around 1980, *The Harp*; by 1986, *Harpeth Notes*. Name and format have changed from time to time, its most recent version being largely online, but a newsletter has continued to be published. Currently we have an email newsletter, a website, and several Facebook pages.

WOC sponsored a horse show at Charlie Anderson's farm on Old Hickory Boulevard to raise money to carpet the sanctuary; they had presented new lighting some months earlier. In 1963 the ever cautious Harpeth did not embrace the new Covenant Life Curriculum for Sunday School until it had been carefully studied by the Session. Session sent a resolution to the Presbytery, Synod, and General Assembly with a copy to the National Council of Churches stating Harpeth's opposition to the Supreme Court Ruling on Prayer in Schools.

The church offered its facilities and other assistance to the Battle Rodes family when they lost their home to fire. They had shared their Great Hall for many services and they would welcome us again once they had rebuilt.

Memories of Harpeth: Harry Halley

(From an oral presentation 1976) The other day I was fortunate enough to stay up with one of the classes upstairs. It was this room up here, Ginger Steele's class, and they were making a timeline of the church; they had a big roll of white graph paper and a big red line down the center with all the dates and little drawings of the buildings and everything, pertinent history to this church. And I saw 1948 there and I said well, there I am. And for the last two or three days since I found out I had to get up here I've been thinking about that… I remember our youth groups used to have possum hunts. That was a high point of the year to me. We went out to the Dickinson's Montpier Farm on Old Natchez Trace and spent all night chasing possums or if we were lucky, coons. And I think I developed a good trait there. We had to go up these tall trees. I was going up a tall tree (it was about this big around) and I had to hug it because there wasn't any limbs. But I got up in the top and I didn't see him but I could smell him. Then somebody put a spotlight on the possum up there. That's one of my memories. Luckily he didn't take my hand

Memories of Harpeth: Buck Jones

Buck Jones recalled the McKays and the Ralstons among his Sunday school teachers and youth group leaders. The young people compared notes on which mothers provided the best Sunday suppers. Lewis Steele brought car loads of area children for the meetings so there was always a crowd. Priestley Miller liked Double Cola and Ne-Hi products which were stored in the furnace room and cooled in the kitchen refrigerator as needed. Buck Jones also remembers the Christmas Tree having been where the choir room is in 2011. When he was a child, it was in the recently completed Fellowship Hall. Santa arrived down the stairs into the hallway behind the Sanctuary and Lewis Steele stood guard at the bottom of those stairs to see that no curious children went up to meet him.

But when the educational building was completed the program moved there. For fifteen years Margaret Sawyer, as teacher of the Primary Sunday School class, directed her classes in a

Emma Mai Ring "supervises" Elizabeth Gaines, Ginger Steele, and Mary Lynn Glymp in trimming the Christmas tree.

small program of music and recitation given in the fellowship hall on a night shortly before Christmas. She especially remembered a candle pageant (probably because of the added stress of mixing children with fire). This program was a continuation of the community tree that Harpeth had provided since before 1900. Ned Ring, Glenn Jones, or some other adult, took the youth on an outing in the neighborhood to find the perfect cedar. Miss Emma Mai Ring was still honorary leader of the trimming of this tree as she would be through 1969. She had been the Youth teacher and leader as long as anyone could remember. She guided them in making old fashioned decorations and trimming the tree which was placed beside the pass-thru into the kitchen. Just as Miss Margaret's program concluded, Lewis Steele started leading the children in 'singing in Santa Claus' by singing one more and then another verse of Jingle Bells until the old elf arrived. Alex Steele usually had the 'starring role'. Porter McKay

Steve, Barbara and Dana Williamson at the 1965 Men's Club Picnic.

helped on at least one occasion and, being less portly than Alex, nearly lost Santa's pants. Sunday School teachers prepared stockings and gifts for the children. At least once they were given oranges that had peppermint sticks inserted in them for straws! As in earlier times, not just the children's families of the congregation but many others from the community came to this program to catch the spirit of Christmas from the children's joy.

In the early '60's, Men of the Church was a very active organization. Eula Bolajack prepared dinner for their monthly meetings in the fellowship hall. They participated in the canvassing of new neighborhoods. They held an annual church picnic and entertained with a February 'Ladies Night Out' where Albert Merville provided the entertainment by bringing hats from his Nashville shop. He would call up the ladies, one at a time to be fitted with one of the hats he brought. The crowd always applauded. A couple of hats were given as door prizes. It is a tribute to Albert's talent that every woman always felt complimented by his choice of hat for her to model.

Gay Nineties suppers were now held in the new Fellowship Hall. The fellowship between the visitors from Martha O'Bryan and our members was a warm part of the evening but eventually the crowd became so large that only Harpeth members who were serving would fit into the room.

In 1965, there were eighteen college students; their

Albert Merville, The Hat Man, was a delightful curmudgeon, generous in his support of Priestley Miller and of Harpeth.

activities were reported in the newsletter. At Christmas there was a breakfast for them and a dance was held jointly with the current Senior Highs. Priestley Miller's youth 'possum hunt' had evolved into a fall hayride for the youth in Bob Ring's Dodge farm dump truck.

Memories of Harpeth: Harry Halley

Christmas parties were another big thing. They were a highlight of the year and I remember, it must have been at the point when I had some doubts about Santa Claus, but someone was with me and we heard that Santa Claus, after the party, had retreated upstairs. So we hustled on upstairs and we found Santa behind a door and we ended up in a lot of hot water. My friend and I pushed on the door and we did get to see a red arm with some white around the edge of it. He wasn't a jolly little elf. He must have been pretty big and strong because we couldn't get the door open.

Memories of Harpeth: Bill Bradley

One morning in the late '60's in the adult Sunday School class led by Mrs. Louis Steele, Mrs. Steele asked why Moses balked at the burning bush when God directed him to go to Egypt. The question was answered around the room. When it came to me, I speculated that in those days people thought there existed a local god at every mountain, valley and major crossroads and Moses thought the voice from the bush was a local god without power in Egypt. Hearing such a non-biblical answer, the room fell silent. Everyone just stared at me. Mrs. Annie was a stern and forceful woman and she glared at me with a frown on her face. After a few moments that seemed like days, I finally said, "Are you going to excommunicate me?" Without a smile she said, "No, but we will pray for you."

In 1966, women first became eligible for the offices of deacon and elder. In 1969, Annie Steele allowed her name to be placed on the ballot for deacon but she was not elected. Harpeth was not quite ready for so much progress. Lewis Steele retired after almost twenty years as Sunday School Superintendent. He would not in any way slow down in his support of Harpeth's work or his interest in the children. Every Sunday morning he continued to go through the halls with the hand-held chimes announcing the end of Sunday school and he was known to reduce pre-school classes to helpless giggles with his visits. Being tickled and called a 'polecat' by Mr. Steele was a high honor in that circle.

In 1967, Boy Scout troop 43 was organized at Harpeth on June 30 with eight charter members; by year's end, they had grown to seventeen. Leaders Scott Paschall and Leonard Mika of our congregation were grateful for the church's assistance in bringing scouting to this area for the first time. Though that troop later disbanded, another came to take its place. In observance of their twenty years of service to Harpeth, Mr. and Mrs. Miller were sent on a three week summer tour of Europe and the Holy Land by members of the church. When they returned, the Millers gave a stirring account of their adventures, especially in the Holy Land.

On January 23, 1969, Priestley Miller died suddenly of a heart attack. His service was held at Harpeth on January 25. Former Governor Gordon Browning, Sacred Harp singers, members of the State Pardons and Parole Board on which he had served, and countless others swelled the crowd to overflowing. Harpeth had never had to think of a Pulpit Search Committee; they were not even sure where the light bulbs were kept! Remember, Priestley Miller had been the choir director, too! Leonard

The chime's mellow tone said, "Time to wrap up Sunday School." It also announced at fellowship dinners, "Time for the blessing so the meal can start."

Mika was Clerk of the Session at that time and his wife, June, was church secretary. Much day-to-day detail fell on their shoulders.

Dr. T. B. 'Scotty' Cowan served as interim minister. A Scot by birth, retired, and living in Franklin, Dr. Cowan and his wife drew visitors and had a great rapport with young adults. When he left, we gave him a car. Programs continued remarkably steadily.

Memories of Harpeth: *Tennessean* Editorial

The Rev. Miller, just "Priestley" to his thousands of political acquaintances, was by no means a "political preacher" in the ordinary sense of the term, but a man dedicated to better government. His participation in politics was in keeping with his conviction that the church and the ministry should be involved in the life and the welfare of the whole community....(It) started with Governor Browning, whom he had known in Huntingdon in his boyhood,...He was a former moderator of the Nashville Presbytery and had served on almost every committee...He had helped establish other churches and was serving his third term on the board of Park Manor Presbyterian Apartments for the elderly. He was a regular visitor to the city's hospitals to the sick. Certainly Priestley Miller was a man who led a full life and was a friend to mankind. Would that we had many more like him in politics and in the churches and in civic organizations. *Tennessean, Politics column by Joe Hatcher, January 26, 1969*

Before his death, Mr. Miller had been talking with Ruth Steele about his dream of starting a kindergarten at Harpeth to serve our area. To carry out his wishes, Priestley Miller Kindergarten was organized and opened with Ruth Steele as director and lead teacher in the fall of 1969. It had an enrollment of twenty children ages three through five. Four and five year olds attended three hours five days a week for $18 per month. Three year olds attended three days a week for $12.

Memories of Harpeth: Ruth Steele

It was a death bed promise…

Every Sunday for about a month, Priestley Miller called and said, "Is Alex at home?" I want to come over and talk to you." That went on about four Sundays in all.

Finally, he came one Sunday, and he put it all out. "I'm getting three and four calls a day, 'Do you have a preschool program?' I have to say, 'No.' Now, we've got to get this going."

I said, "Well, Mr. Miller, I'll try to get it started provided…"

He said, "Give me my hat, I'm going home. We'll talk about the provisions later."

The Sacred Harp Singers were a group dedicated to preserving shaped-note singing. Mr. Miller had been active in the group for many years and they had had meetings annually at Harpeth for some time. In the summer of 1969, they held in his memory the first of many Priestley Miller Sacred Harp Singings.

Mary Evalyn Miller continued as organist and assumed the choir director's duties after the death of her husband until another director could be found.

Lucy, Dan, Luda, Lee, Elmer, and Lucy Davies began their long connection with Harpeth in 1968.

Monnie Hatcher directed. Then Lela Hamilton, our paid soprano, assumed the role from 1970 until 1974 when Mary Evalyn Miller resumed the dual role which she held until her retirement in 1981.

1963 Sunday School class: Bessie Sawyer, Blanche Parker, George Kinnie, Edward Uehling, Pauline Parker, Berdina Hake, Emma Mai Ring, Earl Carter (Beth Uehling, photographer)

PART III

AN ESTABLISHED SUBURBAN CHURCH

On April 5, 1970, James Douglas Blair was installed as the second full time minister for Harpeth. A Nashville native, he had graduated from Peabody College and Columbia Seminary. He came to us with his wife, Ann, and daughter, Allison, from Huntsville First Presbyterian Church. For the first time, a manse was needed. The Millers had lived with Mrs. Miller's father. A home in River

Doug Blair, our second full time minister – 1970 – 1978.

Oaks subdivision 2.7 miles from the church was found and bought for $42,500. Ironically, just at this time ministers were being counseled to establish equity by owning their own homes. The Blairs expressed this wish and accordingly, the manse was sold in 1976 and the funds derived have since then been made available as loans to our ministers in financing their own homes for the duration of their service at Harpeth.

In May of 1970 Juanita Lundell, a member of Westminster Church, became church secretary, a post which she filled ably until her retirement in 1994. Juanita not only carried out the duties of secretary and bookkeeper efficiently but she was a pleasant, wise and discreet mainstay of Harpeth's daily workings throughout the service of several ministers and during the interims. A talented craftsperson, she led a bi-monthly Arts and Crafts group for many years.

New red robes were bought for the adult choir. The children's choir became known as Little Harpeth Singers. It was very active under the leadership of Ann Blair and later, Beth McKay, Anne Carothers, and John Burson. Mabeth Blackburn accompanied. They often joined with Franklin's First Presbyterian Church for activities or productions such as 'One Hundred Per Cent Chance of Rain' and for summer camp at Hillmont. The Blairs revitalized the Youth Group which took on challenges like leading Easter Sunrise service. At times a youth choir was active as well.

Little Harpeth Singers 1976: L to R: Eve Goodwin, Elizabeth Williams, ? Husband, Anne Cole, Tori Stevenson, Kenna Lee, Mary Alice Gaines, ?, Louise Hibbett, Melinda Hibbett, Catherine Hibbett, Dana Williamson, Laurie Bradley, Suzanne Goodwin, Heren Lee, Laura Warren, Lucy Davies

Little Harpeth Singers 1991: Kelsey Purvis, Lexie Wilson, Will Stinson, Lauren Boone, Dorian Stinson, Nan Elizabeth Waldkirch, Leigh Stevens, John Burson Director, Mary Clissold, Shea Waldkirch, Lynette McDonald

Little Harpeth Singers 1995: Katie Throop, Annie Boone, Evan Speight, Lee Davies, Erika Miller, Katie Willie, Briscoe Kuhlman, Lauren Algee, Lauren Boone, John Burson, Director.

The Nursery was now open for our fellowship suppers as well as for WOC meetings. Changing lifestyles began to affect our evening meetings. Fellowship suppers were moved from the first to the second Wednesday night in an effort to boost participation. The Men of the Church brought their cook, Eula Bolajack, back and renewed their evening meetings. Albert gave another 'Ladies Night Out'

Memories of Harpeth: Beth McKay

Women of the Church: I remember circle meetings at Mrs. W.O.Hake's home on Sunnybrook Drive. We met there each month for several years, being "Mothered" by Berdina Hake. At one time there were, I think, three "circles" at Harpeth with one being the night meeting at Mrs. Hake's home. By the time I retired [from teaching] in January 1997 there was only one group for six or eight ladies who met at church with Blake Hawthorne leading the Bible Study. I began leading the Bible study in September 1997. Since then we have lost many faithful members who were active until the time of their death- Margaret Sawyer, Gibson McKay, Edna McKay, Mary Gorman, Mary Smith, Freda Stevenson, Betty Holder, Madeline Leavell, Harriett Caldwell, and Sally McNamee.

entertainment after a lapse of a few years. For several years, Men of the Church continued their annual summer picnic and Christmas dinner for the ladies. By 1976, the men were experimenting with Tuesday morning breakfasts and there is no further mention of their annual projects.

Mrs. J.B. Murray held the post of librarian, working hard to make it a useful service for all the congregation as

Memories of Harpeth: Mary Anne Warren

In the mid-seventies Mary Lou Spencer from Calvary United Methodist Church in Green Hills sent a letter to all the churches listed in the Yellow Pages in the Green Hills area. She requested a meeting to discuss the needs of the community and how the churches might ecumenically meet them. After several meeting the greatest need appeared to be food for those who were elderly or homebound. John Chiles of Cross Keys restaurant agreed to provide a meat and two vegetables and five churches, Hillsboro Presbyterian, St. Bartholomew Episcopal, Woodmont Christian, Calvary Methodist and Harpeth Presbyterian each chose a day of the week that they would provide a driver. In 2011 Mobile Meals, which has no paid employees, has five routes five days a week covering a territory from Edgehill to the north to Old Hickory Blvd on the south and Franklin Road on the east to Harding Road on the west and involving each month one hundred and thirty volunteer drivers. Harpeth, the smallest church involved in Mobile Meals, has twenty members who routinely deliver meals on three different routes each month.

well as a resource for teachers. She encouraged children to get involved by donating their outgrown books and by using the library themselves.

The Women of the Church began regular visitation to nursing homes, a practice which continued for some time. Evening circle was dropped since a nursery was available for day meetings. The few professional women did not object. In the late 1970's, circles began to meet only once a month and Circle 3 assumed an irregular format as a study group. In 1975, Mary Temple Jones and Emma Mai Ring were made Honorary Lifetime Members of the WOC. In 1979, Annie Steele received the same honor.[xxxv] Women began delivering Mobile Meals, a service later shared by some of the retired men and continued today. In 1974, the women refurbished the kitchen and acquired Harpeth's first dishwasher. In 1976, Mabeth Blackburn, Grace Snyder, and Barbara Williamson led the efforts that turned the classroom adjoining the sanctuary into a lovely parlor. Barbara also refinished the original clerk's desk which had served as the 'church office' from the 1830's until the additions of the 1950's. The women continued to carry out all their traditional service projects including White Cross sewing, NaCoMe scholarships and Christmas toys for Martha O'Bryan. An ever growing project was the feeding of sometimes over one hundred Gay Nineties who continued to come by bus each fall from Martha O'Bryan. In 1974 the Gay Nineties presented a plaque to Harpeth in appreciation for twenty years of entertainment.

Mary Ann Warren became the first female Superintendent of our Sunday School and organized the first Junior Church. Then, in 1974, she became our first Director of Christian Education. After eighteen months she resigned and Ruth Moore was hired.

1970's Gay Nineties group entering our old fellowship hall from their bus. Porter McKay greeting on the right,

Ruth filled that part-time position for 4½ years. Vacation Bible School began to take on more of a 'day camp' format. various versions of summer Mothers' Day Out programs were offered, one charging twenty-five cents a day.

Mrs. Porter McKay had started the Covenant Sunday School Class; Bill Halley began teaching it around 1964 and continued until 1996. This class gave inscribed Thomas Nelson RSV Study Text Bibles to rising fifth graders in the Sunday School every year. The Joy Gift services benefitted from the talents of Sally Rodes Lee. As a teen she had followed the lead of her mother in creating pageants for Harpeth services. Now married with three children she brought her own family to Harpeth. Every other year, she wrote and produced a stirring pageant, one of the most memorable being the Bicentennial pageant in 1975 – who could forget the little Pilgrim Town Crier ringing his bell and calling 'N-o-o-o-o Christmas'!

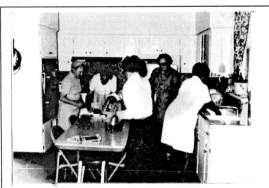

Carol Bradley and Barbara Williamson sneak a bite while serving.

In 1972, Ruth Steele resigned as kindergarten director and Charlene Ring assumed that role. In the fall of 1974, when public kindergarten was first offered in the area, our kindergarten class was dropped and we became Priestley Miller Preschool. In December of 1976, Charlene Ring resigned as Priestley Miller Preschool Director and teacher due to the impending birth of a child. Margaret Hill became the third director and church member

Mary Jones, Ruth Steele, Mary Ann Warren, ?, Theresa Witherspoon feeding the Gay Nineties

Nancy Cowsert joined the staff. Mrs. Hill was well qualified

Helen Baldwin and Christy MaGuirk in the playhouse which enriched children's play 1972-early 1990's. The Tunnels were long a favorite part of the playground.

to guide the program as it grew into the additional space that would soon be available for it. During the ministry of Doug Blair, the church held a nurturing relationship with the preschool, clearly seeing it as a ministry of the church. Many families came into Harpeth from first contact with the school.

In the fall of 1972, Harpeth's first pictorial directory was produced. A second one in 1977 was produced in color

Memories of Harpeth: Barbara Williamson

The Session voted to create a church parlor (in the area where the choir room is in 2011) and appointed a committee of Grace Snyder, Ruth Steele, Mabeth Blackburn, and Barbara Williamson. They gave us very limited funds to accomplish this and we had to go back to the Session and ask for more money. The floor was black and white tile; where the mirror hangs today was a window out the back of the building with an exit door nearby. Eleanor Kelley donated two sofas; we bought things at estate sales and garage sales and then reupholstered the pieces to match. The tile floor was covered with blue carpeting and storage for choir robes was created. We still hang the choir robes there today.

and shows many new faces. New subdivisions in the area were canvassed with positive results. New members necessitated a monthly get-acquainted coffee between Sunday school and church.

More feet meant more tracks. In 1974 Theresa Witherspoon came as a housekeeper to assist Alex Bright

Memories of Harpeth: Mary Anne Warren

One of the unexpected joys of working at Harpeth was the duets that Mary Evalyn Miller and Theresa Witherspoon would sometimes provide. Strains of traditional hymns and classical music could be heard each week throughout the church as Mary Evalyn played the organ in preparation for the worship service the following Sunday. Some weeks Theresa Witherspoon's cleaning day would coincide with Mary Evelyn's practice time. Theresa was untrained, but a talented musician who played both organ and piano at her church. Some days the church would start to rock with the sound of "Mack the Knife" or other popular songs as the two musicians combined their talents, one on the organ and one on the piano, for an upbeat moment for anyone in earshot.

with indoor cleaning. Theresa was a radiant Christian lady who brightened Harpeth during her years of service. Alex died in May of 1978, having served Harpeth with dignity for almost thirty years. Many Harpeth members attended his funeral at Greater Pleasant View Baptist Church and were thrilled to hear the musical tribute given there by Theresa Witherspoon. Theresa continued until bad health prevented her from working. Cleaning services have never been able to replace those two fine servants of the Lord.

In 1973 volunteers were still placing two flower arrangements in the sanctuary every Sunday. Since fewer and fewer were able to provide appropriate cut flowers from their yards, the arrangements were usually bought. Mr. Blair led us

Memories of Harpeth: Mary Anne Warren

Mrs. Genevieve Steele, mother of Lewis and Alex Steele, had earlier begun a Junior Church at First Presbyterian Church in Franklin, now known as the Historic Franklin Presbyterian Church. When contacted, she was enthusiastic about helping us begin a Junior Church at Harpeth. She guided us in developing a curriculum and suggested that we combine Bible stories with filmstrips, songs, and craft activities to emphasize the theme. Harpeth is indebted to Miss Genevieve for her great leadership in beginning this program. The teaching tools have changed, but the basic teaching continues today.

finally to decide that those funds could be more appropriately spent in benevolences. The use of artificial arrangements continued for several years. Another sign of those times, for a while we succumbed to the fad of the plastic communion cup. In 1974, Miss Emma Mai Ring relinquished the responsibility of preparing the communion meal, a role that had been held by her family since the beginning of Harpeth Church. In the mid '70's, Mary Anne Warren became the first and for several years the lone woman to serve on our Session.

On July 4, 1976, there was a Bicentennial Celebration which included a program on the history of Harpeth given by Charlene Ring and featuring reminiscences by many of the older members. Following the sermon, Mr. Battle Rodes rang the bell which he had given in honor of his daughter Sally back in 1954. It rang in unison with bells throughout our country in commemoration of our nation's independence. A picnic beside the river closed the celebration.

In line with long range planning, an additional three acre tract was purchased in 1976, adding to the back of the property. With what remained of the original lot after the 1940's road taking, we now had a total of 6.712 acres[xxxvi] and room to grow. In February of 1978, members were asked to make Building Fund pledges. The Building Committee presented their recommendation in July. The project would connect the two existing buildings with a hall and two classrooms and would add a new kitchen and multi-purpose half gym. At the end of the month Bud Swift, who had been chairman of the committee, died suddenly. Then Doug Blair resigned effective October 1, 1978. Without missing a beat from his service to Harpeth, he had completed a doctorate at the Divinity School of Vanderbilt. Both he and his wife had provided strong leadership during their ministry of more than eight years. Their son Jimmy had been the first minister's child born to our congregation. We had watched him and his sister, Allison, grow and felt we were losing our own. The Building plan was complete and its implementation was under way in July. On October 8, 1978, Sherwood Harvard, who was retired from Westminister Presbyterian Church in

Nashville, came to serve in this interim. He and his wife, Bec, provided enriching and enthusiastic leadership.

Memories of Harpeth: Barbara Williamson

After Doug Blair left, a search committee was formed consisting of Judge Mack Blackburn, Lewis Steele, Ruth Steele, Buck Jones and Barbara Williamson. We flew commercially to Charlotte, NC to interview a prospect and got caught in a snow storm. I remember Mr. Steele, Ruth, and me pushing our rental car down a non-traveled road while Buck Jones steered! We flew in Mr. Steele's six- passenger company plane as well – very crowded with five of us and the pilot. Weather conditions delayed our takeoff from Nashville one Sunday morning. When we arrived in Mobile, Alabama, the church service was over. We had missed Roger Nicholson's sermon.

Roger Allen Nicholson first preached at Harpeth on August 5, 1979, and was installed that evening. He held a Doctor of Ministry degree from McCormick Theological Seminary and his wife, Pamela, was a graduate of the School of Christian Education in Richmond, Virginia. With their two sons, David Allen, 6, and Michael Andrew, 4, they moved into Murray Estates aided by a loan from our Manse Fund. They began their ministry with energy and enthusiasm. But their scant three years with us was filled with many challenges.

A rash of burglaries brought problems. And in early September, a flash flood was exacerbated by debris clogging the bridge supports. The diverted rush of water wiped out a large section of our levee allowing water to enter the sanctuary and rise to the level of the pew seats. Playground equipment was strewn all across the grounds. Thankfully, regulations had required us to build the newer additions with higher foundations. They did not receive damage. There was a history of pre-levee floods but this was the first to enter the building since 1955 when the levee was built.[xxxvii] We had to literally roll up our sleeves and scrub. Having just moved from Mobile, Pam Nicholson knew how to battle the moisture and mold problems. No

Roger Nicholson, pastor, 1979-82.

sooner had the levee been repaired the following April than the City of Brentwood's sewer line construction came marching right down the Little Harpeth River passing along our riverbank. We were unnerved to see the levee disturbed again, but that project turned out well and had the benefit of allowing us to connect to the sewer at no cost.

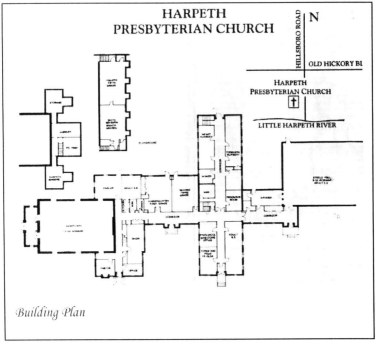

HARPETH PRESBYTERIAN CHURCH

N

HILLSBORO ROAD

OLD HICKORY Bl

HARPETH
PRESBYTERIAN CHURCH

LITTLE HARPETH RIVER

Building Plan

At the end of the year, the 1979 budget had not been met; pledges were low for 1980. Rising interest rates were affecting both personal and church finances and making the funding of our new building a greater challenge every day.

But church life went on. Cleaning up inside and out in addition to making changes to the older educational spaces and furnishing the new classrooms kept members busy. In the fall of 1979, the first of several flea markets was undertaken by the WOC to raise money for the new addition and the remodeling of affected old areas of the building. Almost $3800 was raised. Over one hundred guests came to the last Gay Nineties dinner to be squeezed into the old Fellowship Hall. Harpeth had willing cooks but serving that group from the tiny old kitchen required much creativity. The newsletter was revitalized as *The Harp*. Sally Lee contributed historical items to the paper and she wrote another great Christmas pageant, this one around Bethlehem's history. At year's end, Buck Jones, Jim Warren, and new member Ralph Bowles[xxxviii] spoke stirringly on stewardship. Nicholson said, "Dollars and cents are important, the building is important, but more important than that is whether or not we as a people are going to use our dollars and cents and our building old and new to the glory of God." In March of 1980, classes moved into their newly assigned spaces.

On Easter, a reception after church formally opened the new Fellowship Hall. The women organized and equipped our new kitchen and church suppers were replaced by monthly lunches following worship. The women worked with Church Women United and the Women's Emergency Shelter but contributed to White Cross only monetarily. The younger members' lifestyles did not allow for days of communal sewing at the church. We shared our new facilities with the Sacred Harp Singers in April, the West End YMCA for the summer, and new Scout troops year-round. John MaGuirk led in the founding of Scout Troop 93. Lee Martin helped, and his wife, Beverly, led a Girl Scout troop that met here, too. Classes for adults were going on all the time-- Bible, of course, but others – for example, CPR, art, and flower arranging. In September the preschool expanded to three classes and the Fellowship Hall was formally dedicated. In November the first church wide Thanksgiving dinner was held: Turkey, dressing, and roll cooks were assigned and attendees brought sides and desserts. Always held in the week before Thanksgiving, this dinner has become an annual event with occasional changes in format

By scraping, we lowered our mortgage to $144,000 but the rate was now 13%! Lewis Steele wrote an article in

Memories of Harpeth: Barbara Williamson

On Garage Sales: People emptied their basements, attics, closets and the entire community would attend. Steele Hall (which was a basketball court then) looked more like Wal-Mart with everything from motorcycles to baby clothes for sale. The pre-school rooms were filled with clothes- even arcas for dressing rooms were provided and Ruth Steele made her famous chili which was sold along with baked goods.

The Harp encouraging every Christian after caring for his family to leave at least 10% of his estate to Harpeth or some other church ministry.

1981 began with a Twelfth Night Dinner at the Battle Rodes home. Youth were very active throughout this year using every means to fund their mission trip to Mountain TOP. In thanks for the WOC's providing their regular Sunday night suppers, the youth fed the WOC one Sunday night! The WOC worked tirelessly, contributing to the building fund and to new landscaping done by Harry Halley, who had grown up at Harpeth and studied horticulture at UT Knoxville. Ruth Moore resigned as Director of Christian Education; several members either resigned or moved themselves to the inactive list in reaction to more 'liberal' directions in the denomination. Roger had led us to use homemade bread for Communion rather than the traditional unleavened bread and to invite all baptized children to the table, not just communicants. Now we were asked to add "descended into hell" back into the Apostles' Creed! No older members could remember its ever having been said at Harpeth. Much discussion and research revealed that some random Southern churches left it out for no explained reason.

Emma Mai Ring

Mary Evalyn Miller retired as organist after thirty-three years of service. She told that she first played for Harpeth when she and Priestley met with nineteen of Harpeth's members in Miss Emma Mai Ring's home in 1948 for him to receive his call. She had served without pay for the twenty years of her husband's ministry and, in the ensuing thirteen years, had often served the dual role of organist/director. The church gave her a car as a parting gift. Annette Sparks was hired for the position.

1981 wound down with the annual Youth hayride in the back of Bob Ring's farm dump truck, an attendance of 112 at the Thanksgiving dinner, a 94th birthday dinner for Miss Emma Mai Ring who was still teaching Sunday School, and a Money Tree at Christmas for our housekeeper, Theresa Witherspoon.

As in 1981, 1982 opened with an Epiphany Supper at the Rodes home. In February, Ray Luther came as organist/choir director; choir practice changed from Thursday to Wednesday night.[xxxix] By fall, Luther was promoting the purchase of a new organ, citing flood damage and obsolescence. Beth McKay and Carolyn Stalcup were leading Children's and Youth Choirs. In April we hosted the Sacred Harp Singers and Presbytery met with us for only the third time in our history. We had five members currently serving on Presbytery boards and committees. The recycling concept was first mentioned in that Lewis Steele was leading us to collect aluminum cans. Among new members in 1982 was Mary Ann Sugg, returning to Harpeth after 15 years as a social worker in New York. The May covered dish luncheon honored recent graduates Tom Gorman, Kathy Nixon, and Dana Williamson. Luda Davies and Gwen Swift, young women who had grown up in our church, having led a preschool class successfully, took on the Youth Group with enthusiasm. There were frequent meetings at the Rodes Party Barn, a Walk for Hunger, the annual Ring Halloween Hayride. The Williamson County Recreation Department used our facilities for their area summer program. Brentwood Covenant and Franklin First Presbyterian churches joined us in a four-night format for a family Vacation Bible School.

Interest on our mortgage had risen to an astronomical 16%. Roger Nicholson resigned to work as Coordinator of Campus Ministries in Richmond, Virginia. His last sermon was July 11, 1982. He had led us through a difficult time.

Memories of Harpeth: Laura Dreher

On Ring Hayrides: Mr. Ring used to come to church and pick up the youth group in his big truck. The brave ones would stand up all the way down Hillsboro Road to the Ring's farm, even so brave as to stand up as we went over this rickety bridge that had two boards that Mr. Ring had to hit perfectly or I was convinced we would end up in the river! When we got to their farm, he would slowly lift the bed of his truck and we would all tumble out laughing. What a great time and memory!!! Bonfires, ghost stories and lots of fun happened at their farm when I was little and still today! Thanks Mr. and Mrs. Ring!!!

Many people filled Harpeth's pulpit until Oct. 4, 1982 when Rev. Randell Boone became interim minister and was welcomed with a covered dish lunch. He had been at a church in Auburn, Kentucky, and was studying for his doctorate at Vanderbilt Divinity School. Added to the usual congregational and service activities was a coffee and doughnut time between Sunday School and worship. We shared in the joy of Lewis and Annie Steele when their younger son,

Randell Boone, Pastor, 1983-88

Donald, was installed as a minister of a Presbyterian Church in Charleston, West Virginia. Their older son Lewis, Jr., was already a church musician, and his wife is a concert organist.

Memories of Harpeth: Laura Dreher and Beth McKay on the Steeles

Laura: The Steele family were such strong leaders when I was growing up. If there was an activity going on, you could bet one of the Steeles were involved. They taught us to really put our words into action. Mr. Steele used to ring the chime that meant Sunday School was over. Both Ruth and Annie Steele taught me Sunday School, and I learned a lot! Finally, Mr. Alex Steele used to travel to Guatemala a lot and he would give me coins from there that he had left over from his trip. I called them watermelon money, and they were real treasures!!!

Beth: Mr. and Mrs. Alex Steele in their own way went about doing many things – even cut our grass when my father was in the hospital for an extended stay. It took us a long time to find out who did that!

Adoption of the new Sunday School curriculum necessitated different age divisions in Sunday School. Adults were being educated throughout 1982, sometimes uncomfortably, about the Plan for Reunion of the Presbyterian Church in the United States with the Presbyterian Church in the United States of America. We would lose our Mission Board located in Nashville and other things we held dear. Voting by individual congregations passed up through the presbyteries and synods of both denominations and, in the spring of 1983, the North and South were finally reunited after 122 years of separation.[xl]

In April of 1983, our Pulpit Committee recommended that our interim minister, David Randell Boone, be called as our next minister. The Presbyterian Church does not usually allow this practice. Mr. Boone took a leave of absence from April through October to do research for his doctorate in England and Scotland and to meet the six-month requirement between interim and pastoral status. David Fraser served as interim for this period. Also, in April, Harpeth was featured on the Williamson County Heritage Foundation's Spring Tour. We had hosted the Williamson County Historical Society the previous September when Sally Lee led a program of contributions by the Rings, the Joneses, Alex Bright and others.

Our Scout family extended to include Webelos and the Scouts requested storage space. A Fall Flea Market contributed $1500 to the Building Fund. The Stewardship Campaign was the best ever. It needed to be: our debt wasstill extensive and interest rates were still high.

In addition to their usual causes, Presbyterian Women, as they were now called, led by Judy Gaither, made permanent needlepoint Chrismons (gold on white decorations depicting Christian symbols connected with the birth of Christ) for the sanctuary Christmas tree, replacing styrofoam ones that had been in use for several years. The women formed an Altar Guild and planned and delivered meals as needed. They began hostessing all occasions, including the wedding reception for long-time member Margaret Sawyer on October 15th. Wednesday night prayer meetings were resumed. Covered dish meals were held monthly after Sunday worship. Central heat and air, a sound system, [xli] and pew Bibles[xlii] were memorial additions to the sanctuary. Among new members were Court and Laura White. There were several resignations, at least one in protest of the coming reunion with the 'northern Presbyterians'. At almost age 96, Emma Mai Ring gave up teaching Sunday School as she had been doing since around 1920.

A highlight of 1984 was the celebration of the 50th anniversary of Lewis and Annie Steele on April 13. The service of worship included organ music by their daughter-in-law, Ann Labounsky Steele. Bagpipe music by Annie's Scottish cousin, Donald McArthur, led the congregation to the Fellowship Hall for a reception given by the Presbyterian Women and decorated by our talented Nancy MaGuirk.

Presbyterian Women held a successful Spring Fashion Show-Luncheon-Bake Sale and a Fall Flea Market. They added Hospital Hospitality House to their service projects and kept a food and clothing closet which served both Davidson and Williamson County needs. They sewed new pew cushions.[xliii] They once more hosted the Gay Nineties from Martha O'Bryan.

Wednesday night suppers were tried once more, this time with prepared food provided for two dollars. The youth were serving breakfast every second Sunday including Easter. NaCoMe camps were widely attended. A Children's Story Hour was held on Wednesday afternoons in the summer. Anne Carothers painted a mural in the Youth meeting room. Vacation Bible School consisted of four evening family sessions held at Covenant Presbyterian Church because our facilities were being used by the Williamson County Recreation Department. In October, the building note was finally HALF paid. The men canvassed Cottonwood and River Rest subdivisions. They lost three strong members to death – Julian Wells, Roy Kennedy, and Alex Steele, long-time Clerk of the Session and Santa.

Supper Club: Mary Bowles, ?, Judy Gaither, Randy Boone, Bill Bradley in the home of Jim and Mary Ann Warren.

As in 1984, bad weather hampered meetings for several weeks at the beginning of 1985. Suppers were being held on second Wednesdays. We began serving dinner and breakfast and providing at least two hosts one night a month

Supper Club: Barbara Willilamson, Keith?, Bill Blewett as Santa, Jay Bowen, Beth McKay, Susie Bowen, Donna and John Parker, Steve Williamson.

at St. Patrick's Shelter for the homeless in Nashville and continued with this program until August of 1993. We also worked with the Store Front Ministry in downtown Nashville.

Vacation Bible School took the form of a very well attended Harpeth Day Camp June 5-7. It included field trips to Cumberland Science Museum and other places. The Little Harpeth Singers were again meeting jointly with the children's choir of First Franklin for performances and activities, including camp at Hillmont. The Youth gave a Mother's Day breakfast, had a retreat at Land Between the Lakes, and floated the Ocoee.

All ages took advantage of NaCoMe. The Worship and Music Staff went to Montreat. We hosted the Stillman College Choir in our homes after their stirring performance. Little did we know what a blessing we had received when Pete and Mary Smith and John and Amy Algee joined our congregation.

In June of 1985, we celebrated the fact that we had finally burned the note on our 1979-80 addition. In the fall of 1985, the Fellowship Hall, henceforth to be known as Steele Hall, was dedicated to Lewis, Annie, Alex, and Ruth Steele. On November 1, a new organ was installed, Ray Luther, our organist, having overseen its selection.[xliv] When he became ill, he asked that gifts be given for the organ. On November 10, our minister, Randy Boone, and Patricia Tarpey were married at Harpeth. Pat had been singing with our choir for some time. She had sung professionally and was a skillful maker of costumes. She was working with ASCAP at the time of their marriage. She and Randy both sang in Nashville's Symphony Chorale and added much to the quality of Harpeth's music.

On February 2, 1986, our new organ was dedicated with a recital by Martha Hobson. We were again having our potluck meals after church with only an occasional Wednesday night supper. The Sacred Harp group met once more in Priestley Miller's memory. Our oldest member, Emma Mai Ring, died on April 4. She had been born into this congregation on December 3, 1887.

For the first time we tried changing the worship hours in the summer – 9:00 for Sunday School and 10:15 for worship. As part of Tennessee's Homecoming 1986, Harpeth celebrated its 175th year. A plaque was placed on the wall facing the river in remembrance of those who were buried in unmarked graves on our grounds. Framed cross-stich pictures showing the history of our building were placed in the Narthex. Men were continuing their monthly Prayer Breakfasts. They made wooden toys for Martha O'Bryan. Jim Krahenbill, who had come in the fall as associate pastor to allow Randy Boone more time to work on his doctorate,

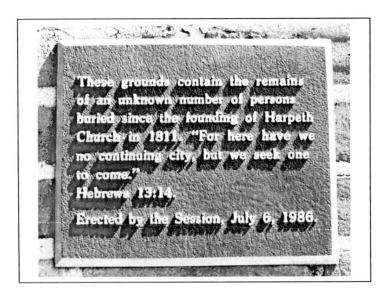

Cross-stich interpretations of our church's growth made by Women of the Church

was an accomplished woodworker and, with Pete Smith, led these projects. Pete's woodworking talent may still be seen in countless small projects around our church. Priscilla Stevens became our librarian.

In August, John Burson began substituting as organist because of the illness of Ray Luther. The Carothers family moved away, and Patricia Boone took the place of Anne Carothers leading the Little Harpeth Singers. Mabeth Blackburn and Beth McKay continued to work with the group. On December 4, Ray Luther died of leukemia. In his time he had led us in obtaining a fine new organ, thrilled us with the music he could bring from it, and held the choir to high standards, purging our files of music he deemed unworthy of our talents. Early in 1987, John Burson became organist, and Pat Boone accepted the position of choir director. A new piano was given by the choir and other members in memory of Ray Luther, Gene Buchanan and Harry Moore. It was dedicated on July 19 with a recital by John Burson. The choir received from Frank Matter new black robes[xlv] which were worn with the white surplices we had used as summer robes since Lela Hamilton's years as director.

Vacation Bible School seemed to have settled into the form of Harpeth Day Camp. There was a Harpeth River Walk for all sixth grade and above in June, one of the few modern times when Harpeth members have ventured over the levee to explore that defining boundary that continues to do so much to shape our history. Junior Church expanded to include third Sunday along with the second and fourth. Mary Ann Warren was again Sunday School Superintendent. Priestley Miller Preschool, under the leadership of member Donna Blewett, asked for and was granted space for a fifth classroom.

Covered walkway designed by Scott Wilson for the congregation and the preschool.

Greater Pleasant View Baptist Church was included in our Community Easter Services, and they invited us to their Homecoming, at which Randy Boone preached. Jim Krahenbill had extended his service through May so that Boone could have more time to work on his dissertation. Harpeth began delivering pies to the homes of our visitors as an outreach to prospective members. There was again an outdoor Communion Service in August. All the regular service projects were in full swing. The Session and Trustees were studying whether to incorporate, and they finally did so following the plan of the Book of Church Order and the laws of the State of Tennessee. A November Five Year Plan for Congregational Development was adopted after extensive questionnaires and small group meetings. We met our 1987 pledges of $109,650. Regular Supper Club socials in member homes were well attended for many years.

But by January of 1988 we were reporting a pledged shortfall relative to the Challenge Budget due to some families moving their membership and others just not pledging. Harpeth, in spite of the righteous indignation of some session members, even asked the Presbytery to help fund our shortfall! By February, though, we had gotten more pledges and the issue was moot. When autumn came, Stewardship used the "Pony Express" to contact the members for pledges.

On January 24 of 1988, there was a farewell coffee for Mack and MaBeth Blackburn, who were moving away after serving Harpeth in so many ways for almost twenty years. Both were leaders: Mack had represented us at Presbytery and General Assembly, shared the beautiful roses he grew, played his violin for Christmas carol sings; Mabeth had sung in the choir, played for the children's choirs and subbed as the adult choir accompanist, and worked tirelessly in the Presbyterian Women.

In addition to all the service projects we usually did, we became involved in the Partnership Program with South Africa. We hosted several ministers of both races who came to Nashville and Petros Dube, a black minister from South Africa preached from Harpeth's pulpit on Oct. 23. We hosted the choirs of both Stillman and Maryville Colleges.

On March 27, 1988, Harpeth held its first 8:30 Service, patterned after the New Testament example in that worshipers would meet somewhat informally around a meal, hear the Word preached, and celebrate Communion every Sunday. Through June, attendance averaged twenty-two. From that small start, the early service has grown through the years to overflow Steele Hall. The sanctuary acquired a new massive Communion altar,[xlvi] the older Communion table being moved to Steele hall for the 8:30 service. The sanctuary service now used acolytes; the minister wore a clerical collar and often performed as a cantor as part of the service. It is interesting that, while Randy Boone led us toward a more "high church" eleven o'clock service, he was the first minister who frankly did

Partnership with South Africa ministers, Alistar Rodger and Petros Dube who filled Harpeth's pulpit October 24, 1988.

not wish to be addressed as "Mr." or even "Dr." Boone-- just Randy. Whether it was the man or the times, from this period on, our ministers would be addressed and referred to by their first, informal names.

As they had for several years, the Presbyterian Women baked cookies to send to college students for Valentine's Day. Children planted a vegetable garden to help provide the meals we took to St. Patrick's Shelter. At a Fall Festival on October 29, the Sacred Harp Singers participated in Hymnfest in the afternoon -- the first time they had joined in our program, though we were always invited to join with them when they met here each April. In the fall of 1988, we had adopted a plan to repair and improve our physical plant within eighteen months using a Capital Improvements Fund.

. In February of 1988, the Boones had a baby girl, Katy. The pastor's salary was raised; the congregation was invited to his PhD graduation from Vanderbilt, and , on October 30, he resigned to accept a position as pastor of Knox Presbyterian church in Cincinnati. Our Thanksgiving Dinner on November 16 was a farewell to the Boones. John Burson added interim choir director to his responsibility as organist. Jim Krahenbill became interim pastor, with the exception of delivering sermons. At the end of 1988, our membership was 263.

It was during this period that Krahenbill made the little stools that are still used during the Children's Sermon. He led the younger youth in painting them. Kim and Robert Early shared the primary responsibility for sermons until our next minister was installed in July. Troop 93 was very active. They placed a plaque on the building stating that they met here. But Session minutes reflect growing dissatisfaction with Scout behavior and leadership. On April 1, The Harpeth Valley Sacred Harp Singers marked the twentieth anniversary of the death of their founder, Priestley Miller.

Blake Hawthorne, Pastor of Harpeth--1989-1998

On July 16, 1989, James Blakeney Hawthorne came to Harpeth. He held a Master of Divinity degree from Columbia Seminary in Atlanta and had served almost five years at First Presbyterian Church of McMinnville. He and his wife, Mary Jane, had a 2½ year old son, Jamie. Mary Jane had background in preschool, sewing, and music, and she immediately became active in all parts of the church's program. The Session examined with him our Five Year Plan developed in 1987 and formally adopted in 1988. They found that we were not on track. Acreage and the limitations of our location in the flood plain set serious obstacles in the path of Harpeth's dreamers.

Hawthorne began in September leading the Presbyterian Women's Bible study, a practice he continued throughout his stay at Harpeth. Later he led Kerygma studies at a different time. There were repeated unsuccessful efforts once more to start an evening circle. The women were making fruit baskets for shut-ins as well as continuing all their regular causes. Women's service on new session committees of Congregational Care and Service and Mission blurred who 'gets credit' for much of this activity, but women were busy under whatever title. They once again entertained the Gay Nineties from the Martha O'Bryan Center, little realizing this would be the last visit to Harpeth by that group. In 1990, the group did not come due to transportation problems. In 1991, our women began transporting the meal and the program to the group in Nashville, a practice which continued into the mid-90's.

110 attended the 1989 Thanksgiving Dinner where an offering of $1175 was taken for relief of the disasters caused by Hurricane Hugo and the San Francisco earthquake. The Thanksgiving Dinner remains popular, usually directing an offering to a worthy cause. In 1997, new members Steve and Melinda Sanders began donating the bulk of the meal from their restaurant business, members providing only side dishes.

Ready for Harpeth Presbyterian's festival are multiple generation church members Henry Ring, Bradly Williams, Caroline Williams and Lisa Bradly Williams.

Pre-festival publicity for the 1990 Fall Festival

Dr. James F. Warren and Ruth Steele slice onions chili which will be featured Oct. 20 at Harpeth Pres- and peppers for use in a batch of their famous recipe byterian Church's annual fall festival.

Billy Easley ● Staff

The first fall of their stay, the Hawthorne's were leading the Youth Fellowship with 12 to 20 attending. Until near the end of 1990, the Hawthornes were the main adult leaders with others providing the suppers. The youth did many interesting projects but the numbers shrank. Youth programs struggled until, in 1997, parent Lee Boone and leaders, Marilee Goldsberry and Kathy Howell, found a mission project for them - Helping Hands in Clemson, South Carolina. Hawthorne, Boone and Goldsberry accompanied eight youth for our first work camp since 1981. The youth thrived on projects aimed toward this trip and they returned to Helping Hands at Clemson for several years. The Clemson connection was to have a long-lasting impact on our congregation.

The music program underwent several changes in leadership during Hawthorne's stay. Personal reasons led John Burson to resign in 1992; Susan Eltringham served beautifully for 8 months before her family moved away; Carl Berg served somewhat unsatisfactorily for a year, whereupon Burson filled in to enable the very talented Vivian Montgomery, a concert harpsichordist, to direct when available. In 1994, she stretched us to perform a Bach

Cantata for Joy Gift but resigned to move away in March of 1995. At that time, John Burson returned as full time organist/director, leading the Harpeth Singers as well as the adult choir, until 1997 when Biff and Mary Fink came as co-directors. In 1993, new hymnals were purchased for the congregation, a set for the choir having previously given as a memorial to James H. Ring. The congregation greeted the new edition with mixed emotion. Quite a few old favorite hymns had been deleted. However, time has brought familiarity with new songs of worship from many traditions and copy machines can easily bring back the old hymns from time to time.

The Pastor's study was refurbished, as was the Nursery for non-walkers. In 1989, the twentieth anniversary of the founding of Priestley Miller Preschool was observed. As previously noted, it had recently grown to five classes. It enjoyed a very good reputation in the community. But there was beginning to be some discontent with how much of our scarce educational space had been fitted for preschool classes. If you were younger than two or older than six, the number of rooms available for your use was limited. At the Session Retreat in January of 1990, the decision was made to reduce the preschool to three classes. Both the church and the preschool lost members and community respect in the aftermath of this poorly handled transition. But Priestley Miller Preschool survived. In a few years, with a more carefully redefined relationship to the mission of the church, it became once again a strong program.

Mrs. Hawthorne headed up the publication of a second Harpeth Cookbook and a new pictorial directory. The church continued its participation in the Presbytery's

Partnership with South Africa, actively supporting the two African ministerial students who had come to the Vanderbilt Divinity School. The Community Clothes Closet which we had housed for several years went out of business. There was a Youth Lock In and Retreat. Another Fall Festival was held and 1990 ended on a high note. More than 113 turned out for the Thanksgiving Dinner, which included a successful Second Harvest Food Bank Collection. The Joy Gift musical, *Make a Joyful Noise,* was created by Lois Brown and Beth McKay. It was presented by adult and youth choirs and followed once more by an open house at the home of the Hawthornes. At the end of 1990, the membership was down to 219, reflecting a careful study of the roll which reduced it to only those truly active.

Beginning in 1991, the newsletters would be put into the mailboxes in the hall and mailed only to shut-ins, others who requested it, or those who failed to pick it up from their mailboxes. Two shorter newsletters could be produced for less than the mailing of one a month had been costing.

Webelos had left, but our Lee Boone's Brownie troop was meeting at Harpeth in addition to our Troop 93. Gregg Willoughby had suggested the project as a fitting use of memorial funds for his mother, Sue Willoughby. Gregg, a radiant Christian who just happens to live with cerebral palsey, was chosen in 1991 as a special leader for the first "People with Disabilities and Coping with Others" camp at Disney World. For many years following, a highlight of Gregg's life was his annual trip to Disney World. Harpeth has been blessed by Gregg. Those who have given him transportation or other aid – Gregg's Go Getters – have been more than repaid by his joyous spirit.

Memories of Harpeth: Laura Dreher

Gregg was my Sunday School teacher and an amazing teacher. He had me read out loud in class from the Bible, which I was scared to do. He gently encouraged me, so I tried and got to where I really liked reading my Bible. Thanks Gregg!!!

Gregg Willoughby and Pia York at the Ring Picnic, 2008

Twice more we tried having a Vacation Bible School for all ages. In 1991, it consisted of one Sunday morning and two evening meetings with food. In 1992, it consisted of five alternating Wednesday evenings for all ages. A return to the five-day Camp Harpeth format in 1993 established a pattern that has been followed with great creativity and success ever since.

In addition to the usual service and mission projects, we participated in Habitat for Humanity, donated $1100 to St. Patrick's Shelter when it moved into its new building, and we sent two truckloads of goods to Hurricane Andrew victims. Harpeth was number three in per capita donations to our Presbytery's missions.

Mrs. Hawthorne, expecting twins, was put to bed for several weeks. Mary Blakeney and Thomas Harrison arrived on November 12, 1992. One could barely notice any lessening in Mrs. Hawthorne's service to the church; she was still coordinating events like Thanksgiving Dinner and Joy Gift music. In the summer of 1994, she was a leader in the construction of the large banners depicting Christian symbols

Mid-90's session: Rear: Beth McKay, Mary Clissold, Ralph Bowles, Tommy Allen, George Gaines; Front: Court White, Nancy MacLean, Amy Algee, Mary Smith, Pastor Blake Hawthorne

which for several years defined the worship center in Steele Hall.

In 1993, Court White painted the traditionally dark green front doors of the church a bright red. A practical reason was that the color would draw attention to our building, which was increasingly being hidden by the growing magnolia trees on the front lawn. Justification lay in the symbolism of the Israelites in Egypt painting their doorposts and in the blood of Christ. Only in 1995, was our bell tower

Memories of Harpeth: Charlene Ring

I remember being sent to the church many Decembers for magnolia greens for Christmas decorations at home. Aunt Elizabeth (Ring) always cautioned me to get the leaves from 'her' tree and not to bother 'Helen's' (Goodpasture). At this late date, I cannot remember which tree was 'hers' and it doesn't matter since she's no longer sending me for greenery. Set far apart, the magnolias framed the church with rich green year round, adding much dignity and beauty to the picture of peace and harmony that had been created by the designers of Harpeth's additions. About 1984, both trees lost all their leaves following a bitter winter with sub-zero temperatures. Cool heads prevailed and the trees were not cut down but were allowed to sprout new leaves and continue to thrive.

lighting reactivated after a long period of dysfunction.

In 1994 Blake Hawthorne served as our Presbytery's representative to the Presbyterian General Assembly held in Wichita, Kansas. In his absence, we had our first summer intern, Leslie Glover. Outstanding 1994 mission achievements were the purchase of two heifers for the Heifer Project as a result of the children's fund raising and the work of eight members on a Habitat for Humanity house.

Priestley Miller Preschool was getting back on track and added a Summer Fun Day and a one-day Toddler Station. Diane Schwartzman became director in 1993 and served with gentle grace, efficiency and wisdom until her untimely death to cancer in 1997.

Satisfaction with our 1994 summer intern, Leslie Glover, led the Session to plan for a 1995 intern. On March 9, Mary Jane Hawthorne had surgery for a blood clot on her brain. Her recovery was slow. Her husband was given three months paid leave to care for his family. Mark Brantley-Gearhart served as interim until our summer intern Mike Capron arrived. The membership, under the leadership of Mary Smith and Mary Gorman, rallied to help care for Jamie, now six, and the twins, barely two, and to supply meals for

1993 baptism of Will Ferrelli, seen with Lisa Hicks Ferrelli (reared at Harpeth), Lewis Steele, Kenny Ferrelli, and Annie Steele.

the family. Gifts to the 'People in Need Fund' were channeled to the Hawthornes. Amazingly programs for all ages thrived – attendance and giving grew. By Thanksgiving, Mary Jane was coordinating the dinner she and spoke for the

Stewardship campaign. Among new members who were to become stalwart workers were Knabs, Drehers, Husemans, Craigs, Groos' and Molly Nugen. A major loss was the death of Lewis Steele on April 3, 1994. His quiet but strong and steadfast leadership thoughout the years was woven into the very fabric of Harpeth's life. He was born in Bethesda in rural, southern Williamson County in 1910. As a child, he attended Bethesda Presbyterian Church, which had shared ministers with Harpeth. His mother was widowed early. She taught school and reared her sons to have Scots Presbyterian integrity. After school, Louis was employed by W.L. Hailey and Co. and rose to be President and Chairman of the Board of that construction company. He and his wife Annie were surely God's willing instruments for lifting Harpeth into its 'second life'.

As 1996 began, we envisioned a new Capital Campaign, made plans to improve the Narthex and perhaps refinish a couple of the old original pews. Harpeth Fund was set up as the repository of all memorial gifts, from

One of the original pews still in use.

which they would be moved for designated purposes. The Harpeth Singers were active and joined with the adult choir for several performances. Among new members were the Lees, Neeses, Oldhams, Veiths, Kings and Sanders, all of who whom would be leaders in years to come.

In 1997 the widening of Hillsboro Road and future widening of the bridge in front of the church were of great concern to Harpeth. Bob Ring, who was at that time County Executive of Williamson County as well as a Harpeth Trustee and Elder, worked on our behalf to influence the location of the road and to keep us abreast of the plans. Charlene Ring prepared a three page synopsis of the history of Harpeth, including the presence of early unmarked graves on both sides of the building. By 1998 the State had moved the route of the widening to the east so that it didn't come quite so near to our door. However they did buy several feet of our land which was already designated as right of way. Members disassembled the brick wall that had been built by Bob Goodpasture and carried the bricks to safekeeping before the bulldozers came.

Our budget had grown to $179,400. Our pledges were up 14% over the

1995 Camp Harpeth Back to Front: Ben Neese, Charlene Ring, Sarah Fink, Lee Davies, Caroline Williams, ?, Lexie Wilson, Liam Hall, ?, Danny Fink, Will Stinson

previous year. A Charles Schwab account was opened for accepting and then selling stocks given to the church. Junior Church was reinstated for all except the first Sunday of each month when Communion was served. Camp Harpeth had thirty-nine campers and eight youth. New pew cushions were put in the sanctuary to everyone's delight. Kathy Howell and Lee Boone were among the adults leading the youth on that first mission trip to Helping Hands in Clemson, South Carolina. Steve and Melinda Sanders continued to coordinate the Thanksgiving meal, contributing the turkey and dressing from their restaurant.

Biff and Mary Fink were hired as choir director and organist and began a long and creative tenure leading our member-ship of all ages and talents to grow in myriad ways. Their ministry reaches beyond the music program into all of our lives.

The Presbytery met here in October of 1997, only the fourth time it has done so, the first being in 1841.

Biff and Mary Fink

On March 22 of 1998, Blake Hawthorne resigned to take a sabbatical and go back to school. April 26 was his last service. John Skelley began service as interim minister on June 1. The Pastoral Nominating Committee requested that renovations on the building proceed lest prospective ministers get a negative impression from its somewhat neglected present condition. A decorator was brought in and rapid decisions were made. The simple historic windows that revealed our pastoral setting were replaced by lovely leaded translucent glass with a red dot in the center of each pattern. Only with great imagination can one now see "our Father's world" through our windows as we had in the past. The historic desk that had been in the narthex since 1954, and before that in the sanctuary since 1836,

One of the new sanctuary windows as part of the 1988 renovation.

was replaced by a reproduction sideboard and was relegated to a dark corner of the parlor, as if an afterthought. The parlor's classic furniture, a bit faded and in need of new upholstery, was replaced with trendy 'balloon-style' pieces. Clutter was removed, lighting and flooring were improved, paint was applied, and the overall effect was fresh, light and good for the moment. Outside, the large and beautiful hemlock trees on the south side of the sanctuary had to be removed because they were causing gutter and foundation problems. Mary Ann Warren and Lee Short developed a landscape plan for our grounds, and with the help of the Building and Grounds Committee, put it into action. This work continued into 1999.

During 1998, programs remained active under Skelley's leadership. Molly Nugen started the "Once a Month Brunch" club which went out for lunch after the eleven o'clock worship. Every year we were having more "crankers" for Miss Martha's Ice Cream Crankin', a major fundraiser for

Sue Veith and Molly Nugen at the Ring Fall Picnic and Hayride

Martha O'Bryan Center and a major Nashville summer happening. This year Sue Veith won a ribbon. Camp Harpeth was well attended. The first of what was to become annual fall Hayride/Bonfire was held at the Ring's farm. In the distant past when the entire membership was rural, there had been barbecues there; in the sixties and seventies Bob Ring's frequent fall outings for the youth featured exciting rides in a dump truck. Now the event is for all ages and our suburban membership finds it a novel treat.

Emalie Bent, Sarah Fink, and Abbie Jones

*Anne McKeeby and Elizabeth enjoy
the campfire.*

1999 began in
the before-mentioned flurry of repair and redecoration. As
was recurrently true, there was dissatisfaction with the Boy
Scouts' treatment of the building. Most years at least one
other younger boy or girl scout group met in addition to
Troop 93. New guidelines were adopted for their use of the

property. On the positive side, Eagle scouts regularly made worthwhile contributions to our property by means of their projects.

The Personnel Committee revisited a rule that had been made some years before, namely that employees could not be church members. The Book of Church Order clearly stated the contrary. New job descriptions were written. Jamie Blackburn became our accountant and Jennifer Bent became preschool director. She led very successful Camp Harpeth that summer also. .

Youth again went on a mission trip, this time to Canada along with a group from Fort Hill Presbyterian Church in Clemson. Lee Boone was a parent chaperone on this trip. She was also a member of the Pulpit Search Committee. On this trip, Fort Hill's Youth Pastor, David Jones and Harpeth found each other. David had grown up in South Carolina and attended Clemson. He had a Master of Arts degree in Youth Ministry and a Master of Divinity from Columbia Seminary. During an internship at Presbyterian Camp Skyline in Michigan, he had met his future wife, Carrie. She grew up in Ada, Michigan, and attended Hope College. She completed her studies at Coastal Carolina University while David served his first full time ministry at Georgetown, South Carolina.

David Jones was installed at Harpeth on November 28, 1999. One of the first social events following his installation was a baby shower given by the Presbyterian Women for Carrie Jones. They came with one daughter,

David Jones, current pastor of Harpeth since 1999

Cayla, and their second daughter Abbie was born shortly thereafter.

Another item of interest was that we hosted at our 1999 Thanksgiving dinner a group of about twenty Native Americans. They had been protesting the disturbance of Native American graves by the Tennessee Department of Transportation. Those graves had been uncovered by construction crews on the east side of Hillsboro Road just to the north of our property. Harpeth had allowed them to use our parking lot and even offered our riverbank as a place they could move the remains, had that been the outcome of their efforts.[xlvii]

The budget for 1999 had been almost $180,000. There was no indebtedness. Average attendance for the two services was about 140. Membership at the beginning of 2000 was 224. The 2000 budget was set and met at $196,890.

Youth met in the Jones' home. Their mission work camp was once again to the Helping Hands Home in South Carolina. Barrett Freeman, who had been among David's youth back at Fort Hill Presbyterian, came as a summer intern to work with youth. In June, due to an overrun of spiders in the education wing, our Camp Harpeth Vacation Bible School was held at neighboring Congregation Micah. In September, Jennifer Bent, already preschool director, accepted the newly-created position of Director of Christian Education, a position she filled with wisdom, enthusiasm and creativity until 2005 when she resigned to further her education. November brought Helen Edlin as our new church office manager. Helen was quiet, cheerful and efficient. Beyond the weekly duties of her office, she made it her task and goal to locate and organize records and photos that had been haphazardly stored for many years through many personnel changes. Her contribution to Harpeth's historical records was large.

Guidance, donations, and hard work by Steve and Melinda Sanders brought our kitchen up to semi-commercial status, making it much more efficient for either small or large groups. Outside electrical lines were located and reactivated so that our long-dark outside lighting could once more be put in use, as was the light inside the bell tower.

Among the many new families were some who would become mainstays of our programs – Finch, Clement, Carr, Manning, Steger, Butler and Lang, to name a few. Among those we lost to death were Ralph Bowles who had served ably as Treasurer for some years and Glenn Jones who had been one of the first of the new members Priestley Miller had brought in 1948. Members who can remember those days are becoming few.

For 2001, our budget was set at just over $235,000. In April of 2001, following a careful purge of the rolls, membership was 238. By year's end, we had grown 23%. Ladies' Night Out was well-attended; Men's Breakfast was being re-activated. We had new directories, church decals, Harpeth tee shirts. We once again held a church retreat at NaCoMe. Camp Harpeth with Anne Krafft assisting Jennifer Bent was a big success. An October picnic celebrated the

Choir wearing robes given in 2009 as memorial to Mary Smith
WOMEN: McKay, Oakley, Bowles, Bradley, Allen, Roche,
Gentry, Farris, Finch, Williamson, Brown, Ring, White, Veith, Fink;
MEN: Burnam, Finch, Campbell, Bent, Dreher, Scholl, Schreiber

birth of Nathaniel James Jones. The Fink's hours were increased and they were provided a computer to facilitate the Music Department's expanding number of groups making music meaningful for performers and listeners of all ages and talents. A fund was established to acquire our own handbells.

There was some discontent with the air of informality that the 'early church crowd' brought to the sanctuary during the summer unified service. Meetings were held for both groups to express what they felt was appropriate in a worship service and guidelines were accepted for a friendly and joyful but slightly more formal and traditional atmosphere in the sanctuary. All agreed to try to be tolerant and thoughtful during the joint services.

One of the Hall Murals painted by members for the Rotation Sunday School

Phone and sound systems were updated. Twenty thousand dollars was allocated for the implementation of a rotation model for

Rotation teachers: Steve Sanders and Bob Clement

the Sunday School. This involved training those who would develop the lessons and some serious changes to the spaces where the teaching would take place. Jody Hudson led an army of amateurs in painting murals in the halls to depict the major events of biblical history. Jimmy Manning led the carpenters. Our rotation was named "River of Life" in reference to our location beside the Little Harpeth and to many water-related Bible stories. Children from K-5 rotate through art, drama, media, real world (mission), and Temple spaces for each five-week lesson. Our five-year plan covers the major lessons of the Bible that teach our Judeo-Christian faith and heritage. Rotation Sunday School began on August 26. In addition to all our traditional service and mission causes, we responded to the Sept. 11 events with generous giving. We also in 2001 bought a $20,000 van for the use of the Martha'O Bryan Center. Notable among the year's many new members were several families – Stengel, Stewart, Livingston and Gearhart

In 2002, "Harpethians" – as we were beginning to call ourselves-- were busy with service and mission everywhere. We had more 'crankers' than ever before for the Martha O'Bryan Ice Cream Crankin' and won 2 ribbons. Our

Etta Britt organized the first music tent for the Crankin'.

We hosted and assisted the Lost Boys of Sudan, and

David and Carrie Jones

Don, Anne, Elizabeth and Clare McKeeby

helped the Village Church. On January 1, Barrett Freeman, who had previously interned with us, came as Assistant for

Brooks, Jr.,and Brooks Odum, Anna Marie Allen tastin the merchandise at the Ice Cream Crankin'

Youth and Pastoral Care. He would begin studies at Vanderbilt School of Divinity while here. He took 25 youth to Arizona on a mission trip. Fourteen of these had gone on the 2000 mission trip.

Under Congregational Care, a new senior group was started, "ECHOS" – Enthusiastic Caring Harpeth Outstanding Seniors. They were led by Beth McKay, who has been a member here since her child-hood, and long-time member Barbara Williamson, and have had many exciting adventures over the years. A women's enrichment study group began.

Somewhere along the way, Harpeth came to realize the blessing it has in a phenomenon we recognized as "The Two Marys". Mary Smith and Mary Gorman for years quietly went about doing whatever needed to be done in Congregational Care or beyond, whether holding an official office or just responding from their hearts — cooking, taking meals to those in need, visiting, cleaning, preparing communion, supporting programs, praying, sending cards, offering a smile — leading us all by example.

Mary Smith and Mary Gorman, best friends to each other and to all of us

Some committed workers who joined us in 2002 are these families: Peeler, de Jong, Spencer and Elliott.

In 2003, as highway construction mess lessened, we looked to making ourselves more attractive for passers-by. One of our now huge magnolias was removed to open our front so that we could be seen from the road. The red doors were freshened and given new hardware. A new sign was designed by Brad Coriell and constructed by Brett Heckman. Those outside lights were finally working again; and new playground equipment was installed.

Memories of Harpeth: Steve Roche

I have two lasting memories that come to mind every time I think of Harpeth. The first is of Mary Smith. Mary was a long, long time member of Harpeth already when I first started coming to Harpeth. I did not know anything about her long and celebrated membership at the time. All I knew is that she reminded my wife, Yvonne, of her Grannie and that she and I would always greet Ms. Mary after the church service and chat with her. She was really sweet. After coming for a while Yvonne was invited to join the choir and accepted. I continued to come to services with her and to sit in the same general area we had always sat which was across the aisle and a pew back from Ms Mary. After a few Sundays Ms Mary started inviting me to sit with her and I gladly accepted. At first I did not realize what an honor this was. Gradually I took note of the how many people in the congregation including the ministers and most past and present elders made a point to come over to greet and chat with Ms Mary. I soon realized that she was not just special to Yvonne and myself but to just about everybody at Harpeth. Of course I could see why because I was already crazy about her. Why she chose to ask me to sit with her I will never know but I will always be grateful that she did so. Ms Mary embodied the spirit and love of Harpeth to me.

Audrey Cates, who had grown up in Harpeth, became a paid intern working with youth after Barrett Freeman left us at the beginning of 2003. She led the older youth in many

Memories of Harpeth: Yvonne Roche

Some of the first people I met were Mary Smith and Mary Gorman. I think we connected with them at the Spaghetti Supper. They just really took us under their wings. Carol Bradley got me to join the choir and I am still singing with the choir. Biff Fink, Mary Fink, and the whole choir have been wonderful: our choir is like another family unto its own.

We didn't join for almost a year and half. I used to tell Carol Bradley we were still just dating the church, we wanted to be sure due to our last experience. In 2005, Steve had a heart attack and had two stints put in his heart. One day at the hospital I was in the hall outside of Steve's room; I looked up the hall to see David Jones, Alan Bancroft, Biff Fink, and Mary Fink coming down the hall. I leaned into the room and told Steve, "Well, we have to join now." It meant so much to both of us that they came when in fact we really weren't members. David always says that we really were. The truth is, that is the way people are always treated-- like you belong.

projects that raised funds for their summer mission trip to Camp Buc in North Carolina. Their new fundraiser, The Harpeth Talent Show and Silent Auction, was a big success and began a Harpeth tradition. They attended

Memories of Harpeth: Billie Wheeler

During the summer of 1999, we moved to Franklin. It was important for us to find a church home. We visited all the Presbyterian churches in the area, but we kept returning to Harpeth. The first experience we had was to encounter the MARYS. YES, Mary Gorman and Mary Smith, sharing their love and hospitality with us as a couple and individually. At that time, I frequently traveled to Texas to assist with the needs of my Mother. Jack came alone to worship service. He would report how nice and interested the sweet little ladies were in his welfare and our needs at the time. The ones of you who knew the MARYS and what a duo of love they displayed understand this story. We did feel at home and knew this is the place the Lord has planned for us to continue on our journey with Him WHAT A BLESSING!

Spring and Fall Retreats at NaCoMe. An Ocoee Camping and Rafting trip in the fall now became a tradition. The Youth held Bible studies and assisted with Camp Harpeth. Camp Harpeth had 100 attendees and 15 youth aids in addition to the adult staff. Younger youth had an Adventure Retreat. There were 18 young people in our Communicants Class. Sunday School continued with the rotation plan. Youth assisted with a Halloween Party. Our first Angel Vespers Christmas Service was held.

For four months, Vona High was our Pastoral Assistant while she studied at Vanderbilt Divinity School. The Finks now led eight different music groups of all ages. Men were again meeting for a Wednesday morning breakfast. Attendance at the early service now necessitated that three families share in breakfast preparation. When the Ice Cream Crankin' rolled around we contributed $835 and many Crankers – and had three ribbon winners! A Girl Scout group and Troop 93 was still meeting with us. Danny Fink's Eagle project was to work on Steele Hall storage spaces. We lost two long-time faithful and active members, Margaret Sawyer and Gibson McKay. Under Bill Bradley's direction, plans proceeded for a Columbarium and Prayer Garden that was to be built on the south side of the sanctuary. The first twenty spaces were to sell for $500 each.[xlviii]

We must confess that the Titan pro-football home schedule caused a major change in our 2003 December programs. We had our first Angel Vespers on a Wednesday night followed by the Joy Gift musical and Christmas Eve services on succeeding Wednesdays. It worked well but thankfully has not become a tradition.

Angel Vespers: Reese Bradley, ?, Ben Dreher, Will Groos, ?,?, Luke Finch, Nicholas Veith

By 2004, our membership had risen to 268. Notable among new families were the Carmodys, Barksdales and Campbells. Separate Middle and High School Youth Groups now met led by Melissa Britt and Audrey Cates. Senior Highs participated in a powerful thirty hour fast followed by serving food at a homeless shelter. There were local "mini missions" for both groups in addition to the annual mission trip.

In the summer of 2004, 28 teens visited the Duvall Home in Florida, cheering and helping the challenged residents there. 21 middle-schoolers hosted a camp here for refugee and immigrant children from The Nations Center. Other youth shopped for children living at the Bridges shelter and collected school supplies for children at Nations Ministries. We were now the largest contributor to Martha O'Bryan's Center's Toys and More program. We collected fleece blankets, food, warm clothes, back packs, and bicycles, for a variety of causes. Youth promotion of the Heifer Project raised $4005. Pledges to the operating budget were slow to come in but the year ended $29,000 in the black.

Elliot, Gentry, and Arnholdt girls brought friends

What had begun as a small convenience for staff became a re-awakened covered dish supper on Wednesday nights. With youth groups, choirs, study groups, and committees all meeting before or after, attendance at this informal meal continued to grow.

Memories of Harpeth: Yvonne Roche

My first memory is stopping by the church in January, 2004. It was mid-week and I had driven by the church for many years thinking that it was just a cute church with the red door. Steve and I had taken a sabbatical from church life for about a year after some unfortunate things happened that turned us away from our previous church . I decided it was time to get over it. I walked into the side door and was greeted by Vona   High,   the pastoral assistant at the time. She was so welcoming and friendly. She asked if she could help me and I told her I just wanted to look around. She took me all over the church. When I walked into the sanctuary I just had a good feeling. It reminded me of the little church (Union Hill Baptist) that my Mom's family attended. I do mean family. Most everyone in the church was family all the back to my Great-Grandfather. I always felt good there when I walked in the door.   That day I had the same feeling in our sanctuary.

In 2004 we had considered forming a disaster response team. The hurricanes of 2005 brought that to fruition. Two different groups, one including several of our youth, traveled to Gautier, Mississippi, and delivered, along with hands-on

Memories of Harpeth: Steve Veith

Although I believe God didn't directly deliver the storm which devastated the Gulf and its inhabitants, I am sure he had a hand in bringing together all who have been and are a part of the rebuilding process. Throughout the 5 days of my journey, I took several side trips which were unexpected, yet quite interesting, to encounter. I enjoyed getting to know my travel companions, Bob Ring and David Short, and I am confident that, like me, their lives have been enriched by making this trip.

Billy Booth and his wife were very appreciative and, though they were not outwardly emotional, their gratitude expressed itself in their manner and was plainly visible in their eyes. I felt a connection with these people as they helped us rebuild their home. Billy. . . even unhooked a bath tub and removed it while I wasn't looking! He mentioned that he felt he could do some of the work himself but was amazed at how we all pitched in and got so much accomplished in a short time. I didn't know what to expect from 3 days of work on his house, but with everyone involved, we insulated all outside walls, replaced almost all the drywall and prepped a lot of it for painting. A new door was installed for their bedroom. That made Mrs. Booth smile!

service, the $7000 contributed by the congregation. Additionally, we gave $6500 to the Red Cross for hurricane relief. Twelve of our membership took Red Cross training so that they could assist in Franklin's local shelters. The usual local service projects continued, includeing Mercy Clinic, Graceworks, and Second Harvest Foodbank.

Surveying what to do next.

David Short and Luda Davies hard at work.

Two of our families, Don and Ann McKeeby and Barry and Kathy Howell traveled to China to adopt daughters. Harpeth shared in their journey of love and rescue by donating to their travel expenses.

In 2005, Jennifer Bent, at the end of Camp Harpeth, resigned to further her education. Audrey Cates assumed more hours for the summer, again leading the Youth to Camp Buck (for prisoners' kids) in North Carolina, having a Spring Fling and Halloween Bash, another camp at Harpeth for children from the Nations Ministry and other local mission projects. A church-wide Talent Show was a youth fundraiser. In the Fall, we moved the sanctuary service hour to 10:30 and thereby took some pressure from the early service but our programs faced limitations at every turn. Our active membership was now at 266. Congregational activities included a Session Retreat held at Copelands, owned by members Steve and Melinda Sanders, our Spaghetti Dinner, and the Ring farm Hayride and Bonfire. Our Troop 93 was selling Christmas trees and wreaths. We lost four members – Joyce Peeler, Peggy Hibbett, and Harold Gaines, who was the first member interred in our new Columbarium, and Libby Fryer. Libby and her

Luke Finch, Biff Fink, Maggie and Jenna Knab

husband, Ed, had been active members in the 1950's and 60's before moving away to care for her mother. She wrote one of our early histories and set up our library. Near the close of her life, she returned to Harpeth. By now we had established

Memories of Harpeth: David Short and Sarah Fink on Disaster Relief

David: To my joy, this was the stuff a reality show should be made of... (I know you can't sell it because there is no conflict.) Everyone found they were good at things they may have never attempted, and the teamwork was unbelievable !!!!!   I still remember Cayla and Coley, "We are tired of just sweeping . Can we do something else?" We found that the girls were fantastic with drywall screws and the Whoop thing. All were truly amazed at the spirit of the girls -- no complaints and willingness to do any job...

Sarah: I was going to write about how wonderful it was to go and help the people we met in Mississippi, or about what I learned about construction, but when I think of my overall trip, I don't think about those things. I think about the relationships I made with people I never would've otherwise. These special people are, in no particular order, Janet Butler, Luda Davies, Streater Spencer, Don McKeeby, Bob Clement, David Short, Bob Ring, Steve Veith, Gene Dancico, David Jones, Coley Spencer, and Cayla Jones. It's not that I had never spoken to these people; it's just that I never knew how amazing they are!

a tradition of having one unified Sunday service at 10 am in the summers. 2005's summer schedule began with an outdoor service in which our graduating seniors told what Harpeth had meant to them. We began to have more and more delightful musical treats – Harpeth Brass, Bell Choir, African drummers, for example.

Alan Bancroft at the Ring Picnic and Hayride

In October of 2005, Alan Bancroft came from Columbia Seminary as our first fulltime Associate Pastor. His background and personality prepared him well for assisting in all facets of our program, and he is additionally a valuable tenor addition to the choir.

Our Church Planning Committee had been instructed in the spring of 2004 to form a Building Task Force to study possible construction to meet our growing needs. The Parent Company was chosen to oversee the process with our own David Short in charge. An architect was hired. Melinda

Sanders led the Task Force in studies of our needs; we started "dream" plans as to how these needs could be met, at the same time researching what current regulations would allow us to do. A June report brought the committee back down to earth. We found that we have many "grandfathered" conditions that would have to be addressed during construction – some very costly if not impossible. And more limited are new FEMA flood plain regulations which drastically reduce what can be done where we are located. They made it impossible for us to implement much of what we had been dreaming.

As 2006 opened, our pastor reviewed his five years at Harpeth thus:[xlix] "Average attendance is up over fifty percent, the budget has increased seventy-five percent; we offer many new opportunities in music, education, and mission. Our staff has expanded. We are bursting at the seams! In prayer we have asked, 'God, who are you calling us to be? Where are you calling us to go?'."Melinda Sanders led us through countless hours with architects, contractors, county codes, and people from other churches. A possible design within those restrictions has been found. Consensus is that we are not called to be huge but to continue to be a church where we can know and be known, where children of all ages have a place, growing together closer to God. We seek relationship and enjoy our history. As a result, the purpose of any building plan is clearly set out – to enhance the identity God has given us, to better facilitate the intangibles we celebrate here in a tangible fashion....God has given us a great gift in this church and in this congregation; enjoy, celebrate, and give thanks." Thus we move forward, still beside the river and the road.

In 2006 under a new building committee chair, Jay Boone, we worked at scaling back our plan. A called Congregational Meeting was held in Steele Hall on August 20, 2006, for the purpose of approving plans for renovation within our present footprint. Jay Boone explained the planned renovations as follows:

- Reconstruction of roof and rooms in the upstairs of the sanctuary building that will add 400 square feet of new space for the youth.
- A new sound system in the sanctuary.
- Lowered ceiling in Steele Hall with drywall, barrel shaped middle similar to sanctuary in form. New lighting will be installed with the ceiling changes. Sound system to be upgraded and carpet will be replaced. Lighter tables will be utilized. New space for worship leadership.
- Moving two preschool rooms which currently occupy a central location will open space for a new parlor with the central access point through the covered walkway.
- Widened hallway in the center of the church outside the new parlor area.
- Moving the choir room to the current parlor space.
- Staff offices relocated.
- Renovation of bathrooms for men and women
- Relocating two preschool rooms and renovating each of these classrooms.

The plan was approved and work began on having everything in place to facilitate these changes during the following summer. And other areas were already receiving improvements. Mary Bowles commissioned our talented woodworking artist, Bob Clement, to create a new baptismal font in memory of Mary Gorman. Yes, we had lost one of our special "Mary's" to pancreatic cancer. Her children commissioned Clement to build a communion table for the Sanctuary in the same style as the baptismal font. The Willoughby altar was moved to Steele Hall where its size is more

Baptismal Font created by Bob Clement and given as a memorial to Mary Gorman by Mary Bowles

appropriate. Clement also restored our historic clerk's desk so that it could be returned to the vestibule.

Colin Parker, a sound engineer member, directed the installation of an appropriate sound system in our Sanctuary.

Communion Table created by Bob Clement and given as a memorial to Mary Gorman by her children.

Outside, shrubs and a gazebo were added to the prayer garden and a cross of steel was installed on the outside Sanctuary wall above the Columbarium.

Memories of Harpeth: Bill Bradley

In 2006, I had such a religious experience that I have, each Easter Sunday since then, been in the Prayer Garden before dawn at the cross above the columbarium to pray and partake of bread and wine. Then I go back home and to bed, so I do not dress but wear a robe over my pajamas. That first Easter Sunday, I had not realized how much light shown on the columbarium area from the street lamp on a telephone pole in the playground.   Just as it was beginning to get light, I noticed that what little traffic was coming by was slowing as the cars crossed the old bridge where they could view the columbarium area.

Then, I realized that I had on my white terrycloth robe.

Prayer Garden with gazebo

Bill Bradley grooming the Prayer Garden, Columbarium in the background

The 2006 Session Retreat was held in January at Henry Horton Park. It was announced that all PCUS records were being moved from Montreat to the John Burlow Campbell Library at Columbia Seminary in Decatur, Georgia. Our attendance was up over 50% in the last five years under the leadership of David Jones.

He continues to hold our attention with sometimes humorous narratives that always end with a deeply penetrating twist that convicts and inspires the listener. We pledged to our Building Fund and met a growing operations budget. Our staff grew, as did our music programs. We held a joint Tenebrae service with Bethlehem UMC choir and congregation. Many talented members of Harpeth provided a variety of special music, Bone Therapy, Bob Clement, Bob Britt, Pat McLaughlin, Melissa Britt—to name a few. Groups like Flute Impressions, Grateful Bluegrass Band, and Chamber ensembles complemented the challenging classical programs Biff and Mary Fink led our choir to perform when we weren't doing almost equally challenging rhythmical ethnic pieces. Presbyterian Women met, usually at the church on the second Tuesday of each month, for study and for lunch. The ECHOS continued to have outings. Our service areas included among others Mobile Meals, the Ice Cream Crankin' and Christmas Toy Store for Martha O'Bryan, flowers for Alive Hospice, Habitat for Humanity, Mercy Clinic, and Graceworks. David Jones, the Britts and others often provided Sunday afternoon worship at Martha O'Bryan Center's Joyful Noise Service and the Session agreed that we would carry anyone baptized at Martha O'Bryan on Harpeth's roll as long as they live at Casey Homes.

Pat McLaughlin, Bob Clement, and Bob Britt

Now with Alan Bancroft to help fulltime, the programs for children and youth burgeoned. Rotation Sunday school continued under the guidance of Lee King. Each leader now manned one area for the year while the scriptural units changed. On Sunday evenings youth, grades six through twelve, met from 5 until 7 in two groups with, in addition to Alan, several adults providing leadership and meals. In the fall of 2006, a caterer, one of Harpeth's own, Stephanie Knight, began preparing Wednesday night suppers and attendees paid a small fee. On those evenings from 4 until 6, YITS (Youth in Training) met for activities followed by youth choir – Joyeux Choieux. On Wednesday evenings the Youth alternated between a discussion of a book or video at the church and going out on community mini-missions. They took on many projects to raise money for their summer mission trips. Some of these projects, like their talent show,

146

provided congregational togetherness. Other non-fundraisers like the Halloween Bash helped with providing activities for our children and young families. There were 40 at a Lock In.

In the summer, 20 middle-schoolers worked in Atlanta; 33 senior highs gave a stirring report with slide show of their service at the Duvall Home in Florida. And, of course, many adults were involved in these trips, and in a rafting trip on the Ocoee,

Bill Halley who quietly worked in so many small ways to make Harpeth a better place.

and a fall Retreat at NaCoMe. Bobby Neese became an Eagle Scout.

The 2007, Session Retreat was held in January at Montgomery Bell State Park. Our operating budget was $387,565 and, with the help of a bequest from Margaret Sawyer, our building project was now nearly covered by pledges. In February, we witnessed the handing over of the keys from Bill Halley to Bob Clement. Ever since Alex Bright died in 1978, Bill Halley had faithfully turned off every light and locked every door after each Sunday service before he left the building. He also resigned from the choir. Bill and his wife Winifred, who had first joined Harpeth in 1949 and had reared their three sons here, were now finding it difficult to make it to services, much less attend to those duties.

We were accumulating parlor furniture, new chairs, mailboxes, etc. for use in the remodeled spaces. We were packing up for storage and the move to trailers for the summer. By May, bricks were coming off the "temporary" wall of Steele Hall. In late May, we moved out of every space but the Sanctuary. Offices would be in the Construction trailer on the parking lot until we moved into the remodeled building on August 25, just in time for preschool and our regular fall schedule of activities to begin. Our usual joint service for the summer months continued as always. Choir met in member homes for practice and fellowship. Sunday school was suspended for the summer, and Camp Harpeth was able to join with Bethlehem Methodist for VBS held at their campus.

The middle school Mission Possible trip was to Philadephia; the Senior High mission trip was to New Mexico. Groups attended NaCoMe both spring and fall. Construction did not alter their busy schedule of fund raising and serving. They started their own Youth Cares committee. One-sixth of our membership went on some mission trip in the summer of 2007. Service and Mission continued to support the usual causes.

Alan became staff liason between Harpeth and the preschool. A new director, Mary Beth Carroll, was hired. Registration was slow because of the construction going on just as prospects were visiting, but, by November, all but one class was full. The school continued to achieve high grades on all inspections.

The Duvall Home in Florida where youth have gone on many service trips. All is not work in Florida.

Nations Ministry where middle schoolers have worked several summers. Caroline Campbell, Phillip Bent, Jake Finch, Maggie Knab and campers.

In January Rob Lea and Stuart Hohl became Eagle Scouts. Scouts worked with Bill Bradley on the landscaping of the Prayer Garden. During our construction they had to find a temporary place to meet. When construction was complete, they decided that the new more formal and worshipful design of Steele Hall would inhibit many of their activities. Reluctantly, they left Harpeth for a church with a more forgiving recreation space. This ended Harpeth's 40 year tradition of hosting Scout troops. Thankfully, we are still benefitting from Eagle scouts who choose projects that help us, and we have Eagle Scout ceremonies for young members quite often.

Worship once again included a Tenebrae Service shared with Bethlehem United Methodist Church and accompanied by strings and oboe. The Centennial Recorder Consort played. Among our own musicians who performed were Emily Allen and Bone Therapy. Ash Wednesday, Maundy Thursday, Angel Vespers, Joy Gift, and Christmas

Nations Ministry: Anna Groos, Callie Huseman, Sarah deJong, amd Erikka Elliott

Eve were our special night services.

Notable among our new members were Chrisy and Kevin Brown and Sophia, the Lakeoffs, the Gentrys and the Crosbys, and the Butlers.

In 2008, the Session Retreat was held again at Montgomery Bell State Park. Craig Pope was endorsed

Sanctuary Cross: commissioned by Mary Bowles and created by Bob Clement in memory of Mary Smith

by our Session for Candidacy for the ministry. Our budget of $413, 208 included five percent raises but was hard to cover with pledges because of the downturn in the economy.

We had 300 active members and were taking in new ones regularly, notably Marsha Edwards and family and Judy Gaither, both from the Martha O'Bryan staff. It was great to have Judy, the Bowens and the Wilsons back after several years' leave. We also gained the Allens whose talented daughters had been coming for some time. Some of the things our busy members were doing in addition to the usual were supporting Vanderbilt Campus ministries and a medical mission to Guatemala.

We began a three-year commitment to giving $5000 a year

and providing work crews to Habitat for Humanity. The ECHOS were still having outings; the Spaghetti and Bingo Supper, Stewardship and Thanksgiving dinners and the Ring Farm Hayride provided togetherness. A Men's Club Breakfast was again started. Pictures were made for a new member directory.

During Camp Harpeth, middle schoolers now did service projects in the morning and then joined Camp Harpeth for field trips in the afternoon. Senior Highs worked as aides in the camp. Rotation Sunday school continued under the leadership of Peppy Butler. Youth Activities reached 40 young persons. Their mission trips in 2008 were, for the middle schoolers, to Davidson, NC, and for the senior highs, to Chicago. A sizable group went to Montreat Youth Conference. In the fall, many attended NaCoMe. In addition to fund-raising activities, their service activities included shopping for Martha O'Bryan gifts and making a mini-mission trip to Atlanta. We continued our relationship with the Living Word Church, with whom we conducted Sunday afternoon services at Martha O'Bryan. Their minister, Rodney Beard, preached for us, and we were blessed by some of their musical talent. Just a sampling of other special music included Audrey House and her brother, Youth Brass, Molly Allen on piano, William Taylor, organist, and Emily Allen and Jamie Dreher in a piano duet. For Joy Gift, all our choirs performed along with our handbells and a chamber orchestra. Music under Biff and Mary Fink continued to be an exciting part of our worship experience and for many members – young and old- a source of personal growth and fellowship.

In 2009 the Session again met at Montgomery Bell State Park for their retreat. Church life continued active in all the regular ways. Bad weather in May led us to hold the special service featuring high school seniors indoors and to put off our annual outdoor service until June. Camp Harpeth

Memories of Harpeth: Carol Bradley

The Bradley family is fourth generational at Harpeth Presbyterian. Bill's mother, Mary Loyce Bradley, and two brothers, Bob and Tom, joined in the late fifties after moving here from Charlotte, NC; and Bill and I started visiting in the early sixties when Bruce was a toddler and Lisa an infant. We came for years before we placed our membership when Bill was asked to be a deacon, and we were not members. Lauri and Paul were born later, and we've all been active through every ministry beginning with Priestley Miller. Lisa, Bill (many times) and I have served as elders and chaired more things than I want to think about. Bill is currently teaching a class and was instrumental in the founding of our Columbarium and Prayer Garden along with Biff Fink and the Garden Angels. (Sometimes he even thinks he's Johnny Cash.) At present I'm active with the Presbyterian Women and serve as choir chaplain. Our children and grandchildren have participated in Sunday School, Youth Group, Choirs, Bible School, team sports and all the youth programs at Harpeth for years. Bruce was a member of the first Boy Scout troop led by Harpeth members, Lenny Mika and Bob Oakley, assisted by Bill Bradley, Bill DePriest and Bob Ring. Bruce had his Eagle ceremony in the fellowship hall. Lauri was a member of the first Priestley Miller Kindergarten with Ruth Steele as her teacher. We always knew Harpeth was advanced but were surprised when Lauri announced she had the lead in the Easter pageant. I tried to explain that the lead was always Jesus …… and was quickly

Memories of Harpeth: Carol Bradley continued

informed, "That is who I play!" Paul was also a student at Priestley Miller with Charlene as his teacher. She must have taught him well as he is now working as a Youth Group leader and mission trip chaperone.

My mother, Madeline Leavell, joined Harpeth after moving from Dallas, Texas, where she was a member of Northridge Presbyterian, where Bill and I met, and a founding member of Lakewood Presbyterian Church.

Our son-in-law, Jay Williams, became one of us after marrying Lisa; and Lauri and husband, Lex Harvey, and all of his family, were members until they moved to Alabama. Four of our six grandchildren, Bradley Williams, Caroline Williams, Reece Bradley and Larkin Bradley are now attending.

All four generations are so thankful for all the care, support, prayers and love we have received from our ministers and dear friends in Christ. We could not have made it without you, and many thanks.

became Camp Edge this summer and, as now established, there was a mission camp for the middle schoolers (YITS) and senior highs served as aides. There were four summer weddings at Harpeth. We lost three dear members. Ruth Steele, with her family a member since 1953, was the founding director of Priestley Miller Preschool and capable in so many areas. Also gone were cheery Robin Oakley, a faithful member of the choir and the women's organizations since 1967, and the last of our team of "Marys" – Mary Smith, thinking of others to the last. Twelve of our youth were in the 2009 Confirmation class. The Youth were busy with their traditional activities. Beth Olker served as a summer intern with them. Mission Possible for the middle-schoolers met here this summer as we hosted the youth from Atlanta, Davidson and Shelbyville, TN, with whom they had worked the previous three summers. This large group engaged in a variety of service projects throughout the greater

Hope Heckman, Ben Dreher, and Will Gross

Nashville area during that busy week. The Senior Highs travelled to Mobile for their mission trip. Our college students reunited for a week of work on the Mississippi coast as soon as they were all home from their separate schools. Many of us attended programs at NaCoMe and Montreat Member growth in addition to the usual events included a Family Retreat at Deer Run in March and an October 11 celebration of the Tenth Anniversary of David Jones' coming to lead us at Harpeth. In

Jean Nixon with grandson John David Hill

Jean Nixon with daughter Cathy Hill and granddaughters Rebecca and Ellen Hill

2009, David published a book entitled *The Psychology of Jesus: Practical Steps to a Life in Relationship*. This was to be the first of seven books he has written and shared with us as a part of his ministry.

The choirs and hand bell groups were busy. A new Harpeth CD included musical offerings from many members in addition to the choir. Members who contributed their musical talent to our worship included the Carmody and

Allen girls and father-son duo Brent and Jamie Dreher. Special musical visitors included Emily Stewart on harp and Kirsten Cassel (whom we think of as one of ours) on cello. For the first time, we moved our Joy Gift Christmas music service to the regular morning worship nearest Christmas. Strings accompanied the choir in a stirring performance.

Our membership was now 348. We were enjoying our refreshed spaces. A simple cross was placed in Steele Hall. Bob Clement was commissioned by Mary Bowles to design a new cross for the Sanctuary in memory of Mary Smith. An Automated External Defibrillator was placed in the hall. TDOT Construction on a widened bridge at our front door (almost literally) was making it very dangerous to enter and leave our parking lot or to see us below the mess of construction equipment. The state used all its easement and, during construction, seemed to almost obliterate us. This was already starting to impact our ability to attract and hold visitors and preschool students.

In 2010, the Session held its weekend Retreat in Steele Hall. Since 2009 had finally ended with a surplus, 5% increases were once again given to staff. Our new budget was $420,363. We had received most of our building fund pledges, but there was still an unpaid balance. Congregational care was busy as always. As a bow to the times, they replaced Valentine cookies for college students and servicemen with Starbucks cards. They decided to pay Gregg Willoughby's regular caregiver to bring him to church because volunteers were feeling less able to move him safely. Attendance at the member growth family retreat at Deer Run was larger than before. A welcome station was created at the parlor entrance. The women made plans for a Ladies Day Out on May 1. It was held at the church and had to be shortened as – THE RAINS CONTINUED TO FALL AND THE RIVER CONTINUED TO RISE.

PART IV

WADING INTO THE FUTURE

MAY, 2010 FLOOD

Members and staff worked diligently Saturday and Sunday, May 1 and 2, of 2010 to save and/or salvage as much as possible of our church's contents while the water rose to flood the vestibule, sanctuary, choir room, offices, parlor and halls of our building – everything except our newer educational wings and Steele Hall.

David Short was asked to serve as "crisis manager" for the week. Repair work would be subcontracted through David Short and James Peeler, our current Session member for Building and Grounds. They would interact with the

Welcome to the waters

insurance adjustors and the State. The levee had recently been raised by the state as part of their bridge work. It was

Bill Bradley and the 2010 Flooding

breached by the waters and the State eventually assumed responsibility for helping repair and further strengthen it.

Pews and rails were moved to Steele Hall; the grand piano was put on blocks; the organ just got wet. Our membership worked like beavers carrying things through the water to safety. Soggy rugs, old asbestos floor tiles, and the new parlor wooden flooring were removed. All papers stored near the floor were carried upstairs if they could be salvaged.

After dealing with our immediate problems on Saturday and Sunday as the rains fell, our leadership decided that our neighbors needed help as well and we should go out and help. Craig Parrish and Alan Bancroft sent teams out to Laurelwood, Wildwood, and Cottonwood neighborhoods and, later, into Bellevue. When they got out of school shortly thereafter, our college students stayed in town to work with Service International rather than working on the Gulf shore as they had planned. We logged thousands of hours of flood relief to others. Our Craig and Sherri Parrish developed the CHAIRITY (FROM BROKENNESS TO BEAUTY) project through Double Impact. They were inspired when they saw so many "ruined" chairs on the trash piles outside flooded homes. Men from the Union Mission cleaned and repaired the chairs. Then community artists, many from our congregation, decorated them in highly creative ways. They

Pews were moved to Steele Hall which served as our formal Sanctuary from May until November.

were auctioned as a fund raiser for flood relief.

Before the flood, Stephanie Knight and Ruth Knab were supported by the congregation as they went to Haiti. Ruth, a nurse practitioner, gave a moving report when she returned from her medical mission. We had 70 people who gave hands-on help to our Habitat House. We supported Double Impact, Nations Ministries, Vanderbilt Campus Ministry, and the young missionaries, Justin and Ashley Guest. Regular programs went on largely unfazed. Beth Olker served us as a Graduate Young Adult Volunteer with PCUSA, as Karol Farris had done in 2009. Our Jamie Dreher worked as an intern. Camp Harpeth was able to use the facilities of Bethlehem UMC and it went forward as usual involving not only children but middle schoolers going out as The Service Squad, and senior highs as aides, not to mention all the adults who planned and worked so hard. The middle schoolers made a mission trip to Atlanta once more and the Senior highs served in Appalachia. A group attended Montreat Youth Conference.

Beginning the Sunday after the flood, a joint Sunday Service was held in Steele Hall until November when the refurbished sanctuary was ready for use. The Steele Hall projector and screen replaced printed bulletins. Wednesday night activities and preschool rainy day activities were considerably inconvenienced. But we all cooperated and got by. The extensive damage to the sanctuary had been seen as an opportunity to enlarge the raised area at the front and replace the original 1836 pulpit with a more compact one built in at one side of the dais leaving a substantial central area for movement of the speaker or for groups to perform. The original pulpit was placed in the vestibule where it greets those who enter from the front door and the old rails

Neighborhood Cleanup: Alan Bancroft, Jamie Dreher, David Jones, Jake Finch, Leebo Davies, Danny Fink and Meredith McCoy

were placed beneath the windows of the vestibule. The organ and piano were moved to the now reduced spaces where the choir had sat. The choir now sits divided at the front of either side section of pews.

This new arrangement was put to good use at Christmas as a group of our young men dramatized *The Christmas Truce* in a service. There was ample room for 5 strings to accompany our Christmas choral program, which was performed during the eleven o'clock service.

Jay Boone had led the renovation in 2002 and now again led us through the many discussions and hurdles with the added time pressure of daughter, Lauren's, upcoming wedding to Andrew Shibley in November. With the ever willing hands of James Peeler and the construction and design crew of Brett and Lauren Heckman along with guidance from David Short, we held our first service back in the

2010 revision of the front of the Sanctuary

Sanctuary six days prior to the wedding.

At year's end we had gained new members. Two of them, Dan Schrieber and Melody White, add greatly to our choir. We lost three of our

Base of Old Rostrum remains beneath the new expanded one

flock, namely Leonard Mika, Jim Holder and the, ever charming, Madelaine Leavell, matriarch of the Bradley clan. The bridge construction was ongoing and continuing to impact our attendance and especially our ability to attract first time visitors through the maze of cranes, barrels, etc. that obstructed visibility at our entrance.

Snow cancelled many of our programs beginning in December and continuing through January. Work was under way on projects for 2011's Bicentennial celebration: a recipe book, a CD, this updated history, placement of historic materials throughout the building, and a variety of events.

February saw the passing of Mary Evalyn Miller and the move to assisted living of Juanita Lundell and Gregg Willoughby. We gained several new members. Our minster began a six-week leave during which time we had outstanding guest speakers and great leadership from our Session. Staff worked with extra inspiration to keep us all active in our service to the Lord through Harpeth.

Youth were busy earning funds for their mission trips. They sponsored the Crescendo Band Fest. Their annual Talent Show and Silent auction, with Andrew Campbell as auctioneer, brought them over $5500 and afforded us all a night of fun. We hosted a large group of Clemson students, who came on their spring break to do flood relief work that had been organized by Beth Olker and Craig Parrish.

The Howells brought John Wright, a missionary to Kyrgystan, who had assisted them while they were there adopting Charlie. John and his family made us aware of yet another field that needs so much. We continue to support Justin and Ashley Guest, who have recently arrived at their mission site in Talanga, Honduras.

In April, there was a Family Retreat at Deer Run. Members participated in the Crop Walk. Lenten Devotional Guides were prepared by Session and staff and illustrated with beautiful crosses designed by the YITS.

Lucy King and Sophia Brown

Reese Gentry, Eliza McLaughlin, Jay King

The flood damage and debris are in the past. The construction machinery has finally left our front doorstep. Yes, the river and road affect us differently than Samuel McCutchen could have imagined when he planted Harpeth Presbyterian here on this spot. But in many ways they define us still – still a sanctuary for all who need it and a light on the path of passers-by.

On May 1, 2011, Harpeth commemorated the anniversary of the Flood of May 1, 2010, by celebrating How God Provides. Media came to observe and report our progress in recovering. Visitors came from the areas where our volunteers had worked and told their stories. David spoke of our seven months of renovation and repair and spiritual growth. He reminded us that the Easter season is a time of renewal and that this Easter has been a very special time for us. "It's about new life."

And the next morning the first of our crews headed to Harvest, Alabama, to help those people deal with their recent tornado devastation. As David said, "It's what Christians do…God's not through with us yet."

Crew at work in Harvest, Alabama.

ⁱ Williamson County Old Deed Book B, p.184.

ⁱⁱ Smith, Hildegarde, **The McCutchen Trace,** Much information on the McCutchen family and their activities, including their support of Harpeth Presbyterian Church, comes from this rare book, recently reprinted. It can be found at the TSLA or the Williamson County Archives.

ⁱⁱⁱ Thomas C. Barr, Robert E. Cogswell, Spencer C. Murray, Powell Stamps, George T. Wingard. **The Story of the Presbyteries of Columbia and Nashville from Early Settlement to 1972**, Published by the Presbytery of Middle Tennessee, PCUS, 1976., p. 65 and preceding. The Presbyterian Church in the United States of America is governed by a General Assembly. At first, it had only one Synod, the Synod of Philadelphia. As Presbyterian churches spread throughout the new nation, additional synods were formed. Each synod is divided into presbyteries. Therefore each church is a member of a presbytery, which in turn is a member of a synod, which is in turn a member of the General Assembly of the denomination. Individual churches are ruled by elders who have been elected by their members. It is said that the democractic form of our United States government is based on the structure of the Presbyterian Church.

^{iv} From a paper held in the Vertical File of Williamson County Archives in a folder titled Private Schools-Harpeth Academy, old and new, Blackburn is described by a former pupil, Dr. J.W. Hall, thus: "He says he was six feet two inches in height, rather full than lean." He walked with a slight stoop which made him seem somewhat lame, but he moved with "grace, ease, elasticity and dignity. . . . He had something of a military bearing. A high forehead, bluish gray eyes, an aquiline nose, a benignant smile and very long black, curly hair (afterwards snow white) were his distinguishing features. His eyes – mild, calm, benevolent- were his most striking feature. A fine looking man he was, but not vain.; in fact, he would not allow his portrait to be painted (though one was done by trickery) because to do so would be a 'ministration to human vanity and a violation of the second commandment'.", pp 4 and 5.

^v Barr, et al. Hume is described as modest and small with an iron will. It was he who presided over Sam Houston's marriage and then refused to bless the separation. p. 63 In **The History of Nashville's First Presbyterian Church**, Mrs. Damaris Steele relates a memo by Hume's son, pp. 13-14, mentioning his preaching at Harpeth. I believe that Robert A. Lapsley and William A. Scott, as well as others, divided their time between these distant churches while earning their main livelihood by teaching at the Nashville Female Academy or other Nashville schools.

vi Williams, Col. Willoughby, **Recollections of Nashville,** Part 1, quoted in Clayton, W.W., **History of Davidson County, Tennessee, with Illustrations and Biographical Sketches of the Prominent Men and Pioneers,** J.W. Lewis & Co., Philadelphia, 1880, p. 72.

vii Harpeth was now a part of the Presbytery of Nashville, which had been formed in 1834. **Story of the Presbyteries**, p.66.

viii The order for the pews and pulpit is in Smith, **The McCutchen Trace**, p. 308, the original in TSLA: McCutchen Family Papers, 1818-1958 VIII-M-6, AC. NO. 90-176.

ix Harpeth's early session books were recently moved from the Presbyterian Historical Society Archives in Montreat, NC, to the John Burlow Campbell Library at Columbia Seminary in Decatur, Georgia. The Tennessee State Archives has incomplete transcriptions of these and other early papers.

x Cumberland Compact signers http://www.rootsweb.com/tndavids /cumbrcom.htm

xi Now moved to the John Burlow Campbell Library at Columbia Seminary in Decatur, Georgia.

xii James used the spelling McCutchan but I have chosen to use the spelling which Hildegard Smith used for her book title, McCutchen, unless quoting James.

xiii Graves were said to have been found during the building of the levee. Alex Bright, long-time sexton for Harpeth, told of having to guard new black graves for several nights to ward off grave robbers who wanted to sell the bodies to the medical schools. He told that once there was a shooting of an attempted robber. Some white persons were said to have been buried on the north side of the building but no record of their graves or identities remains. Most of the early church families would have had family plots on their own land.

xiv Smith, p. 312.

xv These are held in the State Archives. Hildegarde Smith transcribed many into Volume I of her **The McCutchen Trace**.

xvi These McClellan girls were distant cousins of the McCutchen/Byrn family and had been orphaned in California and returned to Tennessee. While staying with the Byrn girls and attending their school, Fannie met and married Henry, the son of H.E. and Emma Motheral Ring. Through Sarah Frances (Fannie) McClellan Ring, the McCutchen connection to Harpeth continues in her Ring descendants into the 21st century.

xvii These books are in the home of Robert and Charlene Ring.

xviii Williamson County Will Book 14, p.8.

xix **Story of the Presbyteries**, pp. 106-107.

xx Recently moved to the John Burlow Campbell Library at Columbia Seminary in Decatur, Georgia.

XXI In the late 1980's, two sons of G.B. Harris made a Sunday afternoon visit to Robert and Charlene Ring, recalling having made the trip with their father to Harpeth by way of the street cars and then, sometimes Dr. Byrn's black driver with a "hack", and sometimes Mr. Henry Ring. They said they remembered eating with the Rings and visiting on our front porch.

XXII Harpeth memories of Ned Uehling, in files of CSR.

XXIII **Harpeth Presbyterian Church Session Book** 1931-1950, April 4, 1937.

XXIV Letters in Archives moved to the John Burlow Campbell Library at Columbia Seminary in Decatur, Georgia.

XXV In 1920 Joseph Bowman, Henry Ring and George Kinnie had described the property in this way: "The land given extended beyond and south of the Little Harpeth River which was left open as a watering place on the public road and a resting place for travelers. The ground owned by this church is a parallelogram, six hundred feet long and three hundred feet wide. Upon a portion of this ground is now standing the present church building." Recently moved from to the John Burlow Campbell Library at Columbia Seminary in Decatur, Georgia.

XXVI **Minutes of Nashville Presbytery**, 1948, pp.9, 13.

XXVII See Appendix.

XXVIII The Statler Brothers used Harpeth for a country church wedding scene in a video, as have several other artists.

XXIX Harpeth Presbyterian Church bulletin, April, 1951.

XXX He later became the founding minister of Bellevue Presbyterian Church when it was started by the Presbytery. Harpeth contributed families to Bellevue's founding membership.

XXXI One of the several sewing machines they used has been kept as a reminder of the fellowship and service White Cross work brought as the women gathered year after year in the Parlor to sew.

XXXII One entered the fellowship hall when he came through the third side door counting from the highway. It included all the space back through the current cross hall. The pass-thru window was from the fellowship hall into the kitchen (currently the Pre-School supply room). The first phase ended where a brass strip is in the floor just before the infant nursery.

XXXIII The one later in use for the early service in Steele Hall.

XXXIV In 1861, the Presbyterian Church in the Confederate States separated from the Presbyterian Church in the United States of America – PCUSA. After the Civil War, it became known as the Presbyterian Church in the United States or PCUS. It did not rejoin its northern brothers until 1983 and then with some distress, as will be later noted.

XXXV See Appendix for these documents.

XXXVI This was our last land acquisition.

xxxvii Rising water had caused us to sandbag the sanctuary since then but water did not enter the building from September of 1979 until May 1 of 2010.

xxxviii See Appendix, Bowles family.

xxxix One member laughingly said it was just so the Baptists would see some lights on here on Wednesday night.

xl George Hunt, editor of *The Presbyterian Outlook*, said in January 24, 1983: "Reunion will…lead in time to reorganizations at every level…; it will create a new and different church…The change can be justified only if you believe that the new church is God's will for Presbyterians in our time…The burden is on the PCUS, not because it is any better or worse…but because the PCUS had the ¾ majority requirement for union that has thwarted the will of the majority for half a century".

xli In Memory of John Templeton

xlii In Memory of Carrie Weaver Hadley. W.A. Gunn wished to put a plaque on the pew where his wife had sat, but the Session refused, suggesting a Bible or hymnbook be placed there.

xliii In memory of Julian Wells.

xliv Only Harpeth's fourth organ we know of in its 174 years!

xlv Gift of Frank Matter.

xlvi Memorial to Harry Willoughby.

xlvii Though we certainly did not want the result of this challenge to be the moving of the road back to the west and onto our property, we chose not to join the State's appeal against the Native Americans.

xlviii See Appendix,

xlix The following summarized from David Jones' letter to the congregation in the *Harpeth Presbyterian Newsletter*, January, 2006, pp.1,8.

APPENDIX

THREE HONORARY LIFE MEMBERSHIPS
WOMEN OF HARPETH PRESBYTERIAN
CHURCH,
NASHVILLE PRESBYTERY

Mrs. Lewis (Annie) Steele

Annie MacDonald's roots are the same as the roots of the Presbyterian Church. Her life is and has been devoted to putting into practice the teachings of Jesus of Nazareth as interpreted by the reformers John Knox and John Calvin.

She was born in Memphis, Tennessee on February 14, 1908, just two months after her parents landed in America. Her father was born in Port Ellen, Islay, off the northern coast of Scotland, in the shadow of the Cross of Kildalton. His family on both sides were active in the Presbyterian Church. Her mother was born in Glasgow in the shadow of old St. Vincent's Church. They met in South Africa and were the first couple to be married in the Presbyterian Church at Natal.

She grew up, along with four brothers and one sister, active in the worship and work of Idlewild Presbyterian Church in Memphis. Annie was especially involved in the young peoples organization -- in those days the Christian Endeavor--and in the choir.

She married Lewis Steele in 1934. For two years they lived in small towns in Tennessee and Kentucky where her husband worked as a Field Superintendent on construction jobs. In 1936, they settled in Nashville, Tennessee, and became active members of Moore Memorial Presbyterian Church and its successor, Westminster Presbyterian Church.

From 1936 until 1948, she taught in the Junior Department of the Sunday School and then in the Youth Department; then she taught a continuing class for prospective leaders in all phases of Christian Education. She was, during this time, an active participant in the W. O. C., including serving often as Bible Leader.

In 1945, at the request of the Rev. Raulston, she and her husband began helping in the leadership of Harpeth Presbyterian Church. She would go every Sunday afternoon, after teaching Sunday School and attending worship services at Westminster, and help with the worship services at Harpeth, particularly in the children and youth departments.

In 1948, shortly after the Rev. Priestley Miller came as the first full time pastor in Harpeth's 137 year history, she and her husband and two small sons moved their membership. It was not without regret that they left their very happy church home at Westminster, for it was where they had worshiped and served for 12 years during the transition from Moore Memorial to Westminster.

At Harpeth Presbyterian Church, she continued in a leadership role. She taught in the School of the Church, in the Youth Department, in the Leadership Class and in the Adult Department. Annie was also a member of the choir for many years.

In 1949, she organized the first Senior High Youth Group in the history of the church to meet in the evening.

Organization of Junior High and Junior Youth Fellowships soon followed. She also served as Bible Teacher for the Women of the Church during most of the years and and continues to serve and teach.

1999 note: She attended faithfully, always cheerfully greeting both old and new members and visitors, even after the death of her beloved Lewis, until the time of her death as she was preparing to attend worship on Christmas Eve, 1995.

Mary Temple Webber Jones
(Mrs. Madison P.)

On July 5, 1898, Mrs. Madison P. Jones was born Mary Temple Webber, daughter of Temple Crudup Webber and John Glenn Webber. She grew up in a Christian home and as a child joined the Woodland Street Christian Church with her mother. Many times she attended Tulip Street Methodist Church with her father. She attended Warner School in East Nashville, Ward-Belmont, and, later, Columbia Institute in Columbia, Tennessee.

In 1919, she married Madison Percy Jones, a member of an old staunch Presbyterian family. In 1920, she came into the Presbyterian fold by joining the Glen Leven Presbyterian Church in Nashville with her husband.

To Mary Webber and Madison P. Jones were born two sons, Glenn Williamson Jones and Madison P. Jones, Jr. Mrs. Jones was a devoted Christian wife and mother. She brought her children up in the nurture and admonition of the Lord. She attended Sunday School and church with her family and participated in the Women of the Church.

In 1948, the Rev. Priestley Miller was called to Harpeth Presbyterian Church of Nashville Presbytery. Harpeth Presbyterian Church was established in 1811 but by 1948 had dwindled to about fourteen members. This church was near the home of the Madison P. Joneses and the family decided that their service and material help was needed to help revitalize this church in a growing suburban community. In 1948, Mrs. Jones moved her membership to this congregation.

Mrs. Jones was instrumental in helping organize the Women of the Church at Harpeth Church. She called a group of about thirty community women to come to lunch at her home to discuss the work that needed to be done. Mrs. Grace Smith of Glen Leven Presbyterian Church came and talked of the organization and the work of the Women of the Church in the Presbyterian Church U. S.

Mrs. Jones was elected president of the group and, although she was reticent about accepting the office, she forged ahead and made an excellent president. The women really worked and had a happy time doing so. The church had only a sanctuary, no Sunday school rooms, nor a kitchen, nor rest rooms. Under her tenure of office, bake sales, ice cream suppers, box suppers, cattle-sale lunches, and rummage sales were held to help raise money for things needed. The women painted the old original wooden pews of the church. No job was too menial a task for them to undertake. It was truly a time of close Christian working fellowship for a loyal few.

Mrs. Jones has served as president, vice-president, secretary and historian of the Women of the Church in addition to serving as chairman of all committees.

She was a great person to visit for the church in the community and her sincere quiet ways helped bring others to Harpeth Church. Certainly she has been an influence for good to her church and to her family by her Christian example.

Miss Emma Mai Ring

Emma Mai Ring was born on December 3, 1887, to Henry Hiram and Sarah Frances McClelland Ring. Her ancestors had been charter members of Harpeth Presbyterian Church and she and her family have been continuously active in the congregation throughout its history. Her father was a ruling elder and the church minutes stayed at the Ring home. Her cousins and then her mother prepared communion. Decade after decade, ministers had Sunday dinner on preaching Sunday in the Ring home. Sometimes revival ministers stayed with them. The fact that no bridge crossed the Harpeth in their neighborhood until around 1910 was no deterrent in those days.

After education in Ash Grove School and Peabody Demonstration School, she graduated from Battle Ground Academy (then Peebles School) and from Bellwood Female Institute near Louisville, Kentucky. Returning home, Miss Emma Mai became a school teacher, first in neighborhood Williamson County Schools. Then, after teaching a year in Osceola, Arkansas, and another in Atlanta, Georgia, she returned to her birthplace and continued to teach in Williamson County Schools—many years at nearby Grassland—until she retired in 1950 to nurse her invalid mother. Hundreds remember her fondly as a favorite teacher and take real pride in having been her pupil.

Her spirit of competition shows up whether she be teaching tennis to her country school students, contending with her fellow members of the neighborhood croquet club, or playing an evening game of scrabble.

She has been active in the Grassland Home Demonstration Club for many years and is also a member of the D. A. R.

In the Ring family, where she was the second of seven children, she has been very special as "Sister" or as "Ahnee" to two generations of nieces and nephews. She continues as an active member of a three-generation household today. Her nephew, Robert and his wife, Charlene, recognize the inestimable value of her presence in molding the characters of their Andrew and Anna, now eight and six.

Always active in Harpeth Church, Miss Emma Mai has served as President of the Women of the Church and in many other W. O. C. offices. For many years now, she has served as White Cross Chairman. She is eagerly sought as a circle Bible leader. She took the responsibility for preparing communion when her mother could no longer do it and continued faithfully in that duty until 1974. Until 1970, she presided over the annual trimming of the Christmas tree. History would be lacking if we failed to mention the races to get a piece of her caramel pie at church luncheons and suppers. She presently teaches an adult Sunday school class and attends all church activities faithfully. Miss Emma Mai combines her own unbending strength of Christian character with a warm and sympathetic understanding of the weaknesses of others.[COMPILED AND PRESENTED 1974]

The Bowles Family

By Mary Bowles

(Photo 1983)

Mary, David and Preston Bowles joined Harpeth Presbyterian Church in July 1976. David was 13 years old and Preston was 10. They had been searching for a church for quite some time but had never found a good fit. Mary will never forget the first Sunday they visited Harpeth Presbyterian – Doug Blair was the minister then. She and the boys had been welcomed at the door when they entered the church, and several people spoke to them. During the service, tears started swelling in Mary's eyes, and she heard a voice in her head saying, "You're home, you're home." Mary still remembers the big handshake given to her and the boys by Lewis Steele after the service was over. Both David and

Preston said to Mary as they left the church, "Mom, let's don't visit any more churches – let's come here." The three of them joined the church soon after that. They immediately became very active in their attendance at the worship services, as well as Sunday school and other activities. Ralph did not attend church with them at first because of his extensive travel with Genesco, which included frequent trips to Europe, and he used the weekends to rest.

Mary was asked to serve as an Elder not too long after joining the church. She became the second female to be ordained an Elder at Harpeth Presbyterian, which was one year after Mary Ann Warren was elected. Mary served on the Christian Education Committee for twelve years, serving as chairman for eight years. She taught Sunday school and served on other committees, including the Worship Committee and a Pastor Search Committee. She later began singing in the choir and became active in the Women of the Church and the Congregational Care Committee.

Ralph began attending worship services with Mary and the boys soon after they joined the church. Because of a critical budget situation, he was asked to serve on the Finance Committee as an ad-hoc member to help solve the financial crisis. Ralph led the church through a huge fund-raising campaign, and the church was brought out of debt with a balanced budget. Ralph became a member of Harpeth Church in 1979 or 1980, when Roger Nicholson was the minister. He was elected an Elder soon after joining and served as chairman of the Finance Committee. Because of his leadership abilities and business expertise, he was asked to serve on additional committees. He became Chairman of the

Pre-School Committee, Chairman of the Pastor Search Committee, Chairman of the Pastoral Relations Committee and a Trustee. In addition, he served as the church Treasurer for many years, as well as Treasurer of the Middle Tennessee Presbytery. He remained actively involved in all of these committees and continued to serve on the Session until his death in January 2000.

THE COLUMBARIUM

By: Bill Bradley

In 1996, several of us were discussing burial options, including cremation. One person said they wanted to be cremated and have their ashes spread over the countryside where he frequently went hunting. Another person thought he might have his ashes spread over his golf course. A third person commented that if the ashes were spread over the countryside or over a golf course there would be no identifiable resting place of that person by his or her progeny. Another person commented that some churches have places where ashes can be interred. We decided to investigate.

We learned that the spot where ashes were buried is called a niche and that the niche is in a designated area called a columbarium. We became interested and started to explore. Several of us visited a number of churches around Nashville and Williamson County, viewed their columbaria and were given the benefit of their guidelines, policies and agreements.

By 1997 at a long term planning committee discussing future church plans, I brought up the subject of a possible columbarium at Harpeth. The meeting included Bob Ring, Blake and Mary Jane Hawthorne, Beth McKay and others. The committee approved pursuing the idea but realized that the members of Harpeth would have to be educated and sold on the idea. The idea of a columbarium was taken to the session and discussed at the September and November meetings in 2000.

By the summer of 2003, the idea had gained some momentum and David Jones, our minister, suggested that we be able to show the sincere interest of at least ten people before taking the proposal to the session. I talked to several couples at Harpeth and Carol and I took them around to see columbaria at St. George's in Belle Meade, Second Presbyterian in Oak Hill and Brentwood United Methodist Church.

In the fall of 2003, I contacted Jones Stone Company and David Jones and I met with a landscape architect who proposed that the space by the church next to the parking lot on the north side be the site of the columbarium because it was very accessible and away from the river in case of flooding.

By December of 2003, we had nineteen reservations and the columbarium site and policy and pricing were all approved unanimously by the session. The session set up a fund to be set aside for columbarium needs and the establishment of a garden. There was a columbarium official committee formed for management of columbarium matters including Melissa Britt as the elder representative.

By January 2004, a letter was sent to the entire congregation in the church newsletter and discussions were had with church member Brett Heckman to be the general contractor.

By April 15, 2004, the session had unanimously approved the design for the columbarium site on the north side of the church including a wrought iron fence on top of the low brick wall including an advance by the church of approximately $15,000.00 to be reimbursed with future revenue from the columbarium. However, between the Thursday night meeting of the session and Sunday morning, some opposition to the site of the columbarium had developed. I remember that one lady spoke to me rather harshly, stating that her children would have to walk by, "dead people," every Sunday. The next week the session reconsidered and disapproved the site on the north side of the building near the parking lot but agreed to permit it to be constructed on the south side of the building facing the river.

On May 17, 2004, there was a meeting of the columbarium committee attended also by some of the niche holders in the parlor of the church at 6:00 p.m. The following persons were in attendance: Julie Peeler, James Peeler, Barbara Williamson, Steve Williamson, Beth McKay, David Hill, Jimmy Manning, Cecelia Manning, Lisa Williams, Carol Bradley, Bill Bradley, Chair, and Tim Bent, Chairman of the future planning committee. At that time there was a great deal of ill feeling that the session had withdrawn its approval for the columbarium to be placed on the north side of the church. I asked our minister, David Jones, to wait outside of the meeting until I could speak with the group, and he agreed.

I addressed the group stating my first negative reaction to the proposal that the site be changed to the south side of the building. Then, I reviewed with them that I had been able to, after several days, review the proposed change more objectively and had determined personally that the site on the south side of the building held many advantages over the originally approved site and that I had incorporated these advantages into an overall plan which I asked the group to consider. I outlined the plan on the paper on the tripod in two parts. The first part was the part that needed to be completed immediately which was the columbarium itself, the patio and the walkway to the front of the church, including the gate. There was discussion about this plan and questions were answered. Yes, the walkway and the patio brick pavers would be matched to the brick pavers at the entrance to the church sanctuary. Yes, two benches would be provided and would be placed on the patio near the columbarium. Yes, the patio level would be at the same height as planned on the north side of the church.

The second phase of the plan was presented and included a prayer garden directly opposite the columbarium enclosed by holly hedge on each side and a low bed and a short iron fence at the end. The prayer garden concept was enthusiastically received. Julie Peeler made the motion and it was seconded by Barbara Williamson (and also by Jimmy Manning). A vote was taken and the motion was unanimously passed.

It was at this point that our minister, David Jones, was asked to come into the meeting and the relocation plan was reviewed with him. At his suggestion we all went out into the south churchyard where we informally discussed the site and the structure and the placement of shrubbery to form the prayer garden.

The columbarium was finally completed in 2005 and, the rest is history except that it needs to be stated for the record that the general contractor, Brett Heckman, refused to accept his fee of 20% of the cost of construction.

As of the current date, there have been a number of interments in the columbarium and it has served us well. There is a very warm, congenial and loving atmosphere when at the end of the memorial service in the sanctuary David Jones picks up the urn from the communion table and is followed by the deceased's family and then the congregation around the front of the church toward the river and to the columbarium where a niche has been opened. After additional words about the deceased, David Jones places the urn in the niche and the family, usually each of them, participates in replacing the earth over the urn.

Surprisingly, we found that the spiritual atmosphere was so positive that people lingered, speaking to the family and each other for a long while following an interment.

MEMBERSHIP

By: Tom Livingston

I don't know how long it was after my first visit that I joined Harpeth Presbyterian Church in October, 2001, but I do remember my first visit put me in the ER that night!!! We were invited to attend HPC by the Parkers. Tamara & Colin convinced us, as parents of young children, that HPC had this "really cool" breakfast as part of worship. You could get the kids there (really, bribe them with treats) and the food kept them occupied while you could listen to the sermon. It sounded inviting, so early one Sunday morning we showed up.

It was not a traditional Presbyterian worship, to say the least. Long rows of tables filled what could only be described as a converted gym. No riser in the front to elevate the pastor, no music loft, heck no ceiling!! In fact, off large beams in an aptly named "Steele Hall" hung gymnasium lights, for sanctuary illumination. You know the kind?? When they're first turned on they hum; as they warm up, they quiet down and brighten up. Four walls with very few windows, fewer wall decorations, and a lone basketball goal made you feel like you were in a startup church, not one with almost 200 years of history.

But the service was great! A "preacher" about my age (little younger), with kids and life experiences similar to mine promoting positive fellowship. I liked him from the start. The service was followed by what can only be described as a military drill without the military precision. The bustle of people clearing food, stacking books, folding chairs and putting away (heavy) tables converted HPC Steele Hall back to its gym-like status. Most people went on to Sunday school or elsewhere. I remember then, just the Parker-four and the Livingston four talking and hanging out in Steele Hall. The lone basketball goal transformed back to the centerpiece for kids and time stretched on in adult conversation.

I had to go into work that day, but left after a couple of hours because my head hurt. When I started home, I met the family out for dinner and the boys' mom commented that their cheeks were "flushed" and we wondered if they were getting sick. I noted my headache and truly that "my eyes hurt". Little did I know then that in just a couple more hours, late on a Sunday night, the pain would get so bad I had to get a ride to the ER. I could write a longer story just on that event. The short of it: I sat from 10:30 Sunday night until 4:30 Monday morning in the ER…waiting. I sat (alone) in a wheelchair with my eyes closed, because to open them hurt unbelievably.

Now they say if you take away one sense the others get more attuned. When you can't see – you listen. In the ER you get taken by "order of importance". I learned that night that "hurting eyes" ranks just above a "boo-boo"!! I heard people coming in with chest pains (automatic front-of-the-line), kids in real pain (next), and such a steady flow of ambulances that sometime in the Monday a.m. a nurse remarked she had "NEVER seen it this busy". All the while, I waited blindly for my turn. Finally a nurse took me to a doctor. This guy pries my eyes open like he's removing the lids altogether. He says he's going to numb them. Oh, the sweet drug that does THAT!! Now that I can see for the first time in hours, all I want to do is go home and rest. I'm diagnosed with "pink eye", given a script for drops, and sent on my way. But, as I reenter the waiting room to call for a ride, who do I see--the Parkers!! And man, their eyes looked like mine felt.

I followed up with an eye doctor who diagnosed a "burn". Almost like "a chemical burn", they noted. The Parkers contacted the church and explained what happened. I understand that some church leaders then grabbed table and chairs and sat down in the middle of Steele Hall to see if they could find the problem. Was there a chemical in the carpet, agitated by all the foot traffic? Was it just a fluke that the Parkers and I ended up in the ER? Does a dyslectic agnostic lie awake wondering if there is a "doG"?? They thought through the problem in true Presbyterian form – a committee. After some time, one member noted that he felt like he was getting sunburn on the side of his face.

In the end, it was determined that one of those gym lights had a broken cover/filter and was pumping out UV like a sun bed on steroids. When the pastor relayed the story, over the coming Sundays, more families came forward with tales of their own. The apologies I received and the compassion I was shown let me know the "little church by the river" was going to be my church home. And so, by the grace of God (a more favorable light), HPC has been *my* church ever since.

FLOODS
VIRGINIA KNICKLEBEIN

Psalm 29: 10-11: The Lord sitteth upon the flood; yea, the Lord sitteth King forever. The Lord will give strength unto his people; the Lord will bless his people with peace.

Floods of memories wash over me as I reflect back to the Nashville floods in May, 2010. I remember seeing with horror images of my hometown washing down the interstate while I was marooned in Pittsburg for a beloved goddaughter's college graduation. I remember the flooding desperation as I got emails about my little church by the river. And then, emails and pictures documenting my little church IN the river. There was a maddening and difficult journey to return to Nashville, constantly worrying about my aged parents who were marooned at my home without phone or electricity. Who was safe? Who had sustained damage? How was I getting to them? And what could I do once I got there? There were floods of tears as, with determination, I flew from Pittsburg to Chicago, only to be told all connecting flights to Nashville were canceled. I flew to Louisville, rented a truck with difficulty (and after prayers, tears and a true southern hissy fit) and drove madly toward home. As I reached Briley Parkway, the levy around Opryland breached and waters began to come up onto the highway. I was directed by God's hand and the loving voice of a dear friend whom I managed to reach via cell. I made it safe and dry to Nashville , to begin the recovery process.

The flood brought devastation, loss, and misery. Yet, like Christ's resurrection, both our church and this community have found strength, grace and blessings due to these trials and tribulations.

Prayer: Father God, help us all to remember that in the midst of floods of troubles, you are there. Guide our hearts and minds to rely on your strength. Give us faith when we feel overwhelmed. Help us to seek opportunity to reflect on your strength and glory in your steadfast love. In Christ's name we pray, Amen.